SUCCESS
IS
WHO
YOU ARE

THE BLUEPRINT FOR ACHIEVING OUTSTANDING SUCCESS

SAM ADEYEMI

Printed in the United States of America

ACKNOWLEDGEMENTS

I wish to express my appreciation to the exceptional people who contributed in several ways to make this book a reality. I appreciate the hardworking staff at Pneuma Publishing Limited led by Toyin Olanrewaju, who did the proofreading and editing for the original manuscript. And I appreciate Rotimi Kehinde and the staff at Godkulture Publishing for the editing of this edition and designing the page layout.

It took years of learning and experimenting to learn the principles that are expressed in this book. I appreciate my family, friends, mentors, and colleagues in our organizations, which have offered encouragement along the way.

I sincerely celebrate my dear wife, Nike, who has been my partner in experimenting as we have tried to apply the principles we have learned. Her unusual capacity for faith made it possible for us to take risks. And we have experienced the exciting results together. I appreciate our children for their understanding, as they have been part of the experimenting process. Our future will be even brighter!

CONTENTS

INTRODUCTION

In 1990, I was unemployed, frustrated and confused about life. The idea of the American dream was just that, a dream. There were times that things would look promising but those things would not turn out well for me. Life gave me an opportunity to travel from Nigeria to the United Kingdom, which I thought was going to be the best thing to happen to me in my life at that point. I thought leaving the country was the only option for me to achieve success. However, when the plan fell through I was heartbroken and felt hopeless. This is why I can fully relate to those who are despondent and desperate, who feel like they have no hope. This book was written with a calling that I have felt, to share the principles that have transformed my life. These principles make me feel confident in saying, "Success is not a matter of chances; it is a matter of choices."

To be honest, going from Nigeria to the United Kingdom was the perfect opportunity to change my life by taking a nine-month course and I was quite certain that I would never return to Nigeria. Financial situations in Nigeria had gotten so bad it affected our family business. All initial arrangements for the trip worked out well and a friend named Sam, my brother Victor, and I had received our letters of acceptance. We met the owner of a travel agency through our pastor and bought our flight tickets through him because we felt that his connections would help us get into the United Kingdom. The owner was a friend to a close relation of the royal family in England and was held in high regard by the British High Commissioner in Nigeria. We thought that the man was so connected our visas to the United Kingdom would be given. But, the week before we applied for our visas, something unexpectedly went wrong. The whole arrangement had been predicated on the relationship between this fine gentleman and our pastor but just a few days to our visit to the British High Commission, that relationship suffered a terrible setback. The man decided not to help us anymore with getting the visas but he had gotten the flight tickets for us. When we applied for the visas at the High Commission, the officials asked for some paper work, which we did not have and we were denied the visas.

A few weeks later, the travel agent came to our house, asking to take back the tickets he had helped purchase. "Well, I should get the tickets back," the agent said rather coldly. We gave him the tickets and watched our dream of going to England melt away as he drove off. I was upset for weeks. Life just bottomed out on me. At that point it felt like the end of the road. I was finished! Sometimes tears would well up in my eyes as I thought about the missed opportunity. I felt there had to be evil forces ruining my destiny, and such were the thoughts that would run through my mind.

I calmed down eventually and began to talk to God again. "Something must be wrong somewhere, Lord. What am I supposed to do?" I remember coming across Dr. Robert Schuller's book, *Tough Times Never Last but Tough People Do.*[1] This marked a new beginning for me. I would like to share part of the transformation process with you in this book, about the laws of success that can make life so predictable. Today, I have been privileged to travel around the world while leading a thriving church in Nigeria. I am living a successful life in the very same country I wanted to escape from.

I should tell you that principles (also called laws) govern our world to a large extent. A principle is a universal fact. For example, the law of gravity, which states that, "Whatever goes up must come down." Isaac Newton even developed an equation for it. The law of gravity makes life predictable; but for this law to be true, whatever you throw up must come down.

Similarly, one of the laws of motion discovered by Isaac Newton states that an object in a state of rest or uniform motion remains in that state until an external force is applied. This law also makes life predictable, because if you can remove every force from an object, it will stand still. It is the only way we stop our vehicles. That is the way an aircraft comes to a halt. Such laws govern the world, and make life predictable.

A law holds true on any spot on the earth at any time no matter who is operating it. For example, if you jump from a ten-story building in New York, you will fall down. If you think you fell down because some evil forces were after your destiny, you can fly to Beijing, China and jump from a ten-story building there, you will just as well fall down. The interesting thing here is the laws work irrespective of who the person is. If the President of the United States jumps from a ten-story building, he will fall down just as a poor and unknown man would.

What do we know about laws?

First, laws make life predictable. Second, laws are the same for everybody on earth; they give equal opportunity to all human beings. They have no respect for social status or color. That helps a great deal! Also, laws make power available that we can leverage to achieve things beyond our ability, like traveling thousands of miles in a matter of hours, in an aircraft, or growing a seed into a tree. Then, when we understand how a law works, it empowers us to create and to innovate. For example, understanding the laws of aerodynamics makes it possible for us to create aircrafts. Finally, different laws govern different areas of life. If you can understand these laws then you can get predictable results once you satisfy their conditions.

This book is an offshoot of the fundamental things I have learnt over the years about the laws of success. I believe that reading this book and applying the principles in your personal circumstances will make the coming years your best ever. Therefore, read along carefully as we take a journey into the laws that govern success. Make your decisions and take action with courage. You will succeed!

SUCCESS
IS WHO
YOU ARE

1
SUCCESS SECRETS

One of the profound principles I discovered in my quest to experience a change in my circumstances is that success actually begins from the inside out. It must start within you before it manifests outwardly. Many people try to get outward things they have not gotten on the inside and this causes frustration. They do not understand how this world was designed to run. Whatever will happen on this earth to anyone has been designed to happen first in the heart of man..

For as he thinks in his heart, so is he.[1]

This is simply saying that *your life will literally reflect the state of your heart.* So I say, it is all a matter of the heart; it is *first within and then without.* It is a question of the inner man.

The famous king, Solomon, once said; *"Keep your heart with all diligence, for out of it spring the issues of life."*[2] Put another way, the forces that control life come out of the heart. This is where the hard work is. It is first in your heart before it shows outside. Your state of being on the earth is a direct reflection of the state of your heart.

People want to get an amount of money on the outside that they do not have on the inside. They want to rise to levels of promotion that they have not risen to on the inside. They are trying to break a law. You need a force that is stronger than the force of gravity to make something go up and not come down. So when people try to succeed while working against a law of nature, they have to exert tremendous energy. Most times, they do not get their desired results. Success begins in your heart. You are designed to grow from the inside out. You are not designed to become on the outside what you have not yet become on the inside.

> **The good man from his inner good treasure flings forth good things, and the evil man out of his inner evil storehouse flings forth evil things.**[3]

This is a powerful statement! You proclaim success or failure from your heart. You might be asking, "So, what is in my heart?" Well, you will surely know if you check what you have been proclaiming and expressing. The circumstances of your life today reflect how much or how far you have gone in the development of your heart. When King Solomon says you should keep your heart with all diligence, it implies that it takes hard work to make changes on the inside.

One of Newton's laws of motion implies that all objects remain at a state of rest until a force is applied.[4] When I combine that with the principle which says, *"For as he thinks in his heart, so is he,"* I come to this conclusion: "All progress remains at a state of rest until a mental force is applied." You must initiate things in your heart and mind before you try to apply them in the physical world.

Scaling the mountain from the inside

Your status in life will remain at a state of rest until an internal force is applied to it. You cannot scale a mountain on the outside that you have not scaled on the inside.

> **Whoever says to this mountain, 'Be removed and be cast into the sea,' and does not doubt in his heart, but believes that those things he says will be done, he will have whatever he says.** [5]

In other words, before you start talking to your mountain (your problems), you must believe the mountain moved in your heart. You must get to the point where it is unfathomable that the mountain would not move if you told it to. That is faith, and it works!

Face to face with the extraordinary

I love the discussion between Jesus and Nicodemus, a leader of the Pharisees in those days. I often use this story as a foundation when I teach on success.

> **This man came to Jesus by night and said to Him, "Rabbi, we know that You are a teacher come from God; for no one can do these signs that You do unless God is with him." Jesus answered and said to him, "Most assuredly, I say to you, unless one is born again, he cannot see the kingdom of God."** [6]

Nicodemus was just like most of us. He was trying to find out the secret of the extraordinary results that Christ achieved. Nicodemus emphasized on the word 'do'. When we come across someone who has better results than we have, we tend to think that it is because the person is doing something we are not doing or that if we do what the person is doing we will get the same results. We later find out that even if you do the exact same thing someone else is doing, your results may differ.

Success is first about a state of being before it is a state of action. You are essentially a human being not a 'human doing'. There is a great difference between state of *being* and *state of action*. 'Being' is about your nature while 'action' is just activity. Christ said Nicodemus could only develop the capacity to do what Christ was doing by being born again. Nicodemus was confused, and understandably so. He had never seen a human being born twice. "How is a man my age to enter my mother's womb and be born the second time?" He asked.

Jesus used the word *born* because you derive your nature, your being, from the person who gave birth to you. It is that nature that dictates what you do. It puts a cap on your capabilities. Who you are puts a limit on what you can do. Your nature ultimately determines your future. Let me explain this. A lizard by nature cannot speak the language of a human being. A dog barks, a cow moos, a horse neighs, and a snake hisses because it is in their nature. When something comes out of your nature, we say it is natural to you. You do it subconsciously and instinctively without any strenuous effort.

Jesus was saying, therefore, that you derive your nature from the person who gave birth to you, pointing at the inherent difference between Him and Nicodemus. That is why He said:

> **That which is born of the flesh is flesh, and that which is born of the Spirit is spirit.**[7]

Nicodemus was human because he was born by humans. To have the same nature as Jesus, he had to be born by God. It is only the Spirit of God that can plant the nature of God in man.

Why we have problems

Some people have a problem with the concept of a human being having God's nature. But kind begets kind. If human beings give birth to human beings, God should be expected to beget gods.

That was the import of what Jesus told his religious night caller. When the nature of God meets problems, it turns them into opportunities for miracles.

Your capacity for success is rooted in your God-nature. It is God's nature to achieve all His goals. When God's nature is birthed in you, it becomes your nature to be successful. There is limited strength in your physical nature. For instance, how much weight can you carry physically? But you can lift precisely any weight in your imagination. That is the part of you that really moves things on this earth, and it is the nature you share with God – your spiritual nature.

The power of the new birth

Back in Eden, according to the biblical account, the first man and woman were created with God's nature. But when they disobeyed God, God's nature in them died and man took on the nature of sin. However, when we accept the death and resurrection of Jesus Christ as done on our behalf, our sins are forgiven. The power of the Holy Spirit comes into one's life and re-creates the heart, imparting the nature of God. The moment you become born again you cease to be an ordinary person. You inherit the God-nature, because you are born by the Spirit of God. See how Jesus stakes a claim on this:

> "...I and My Father are one." Then the Jews took up stones again to stone Him. Jesus answered them, "Many good works I have shown you from My Father. For which of those works do you stone Me?" The Jews answered Him, saying, "For a good work we do not stone You, but for blasphemy, and because You, being a Man, make Yourself God." [8]

What Jesus claimed to be, to the Jews, was unimaginable. He said that God was His Father, and the people knew the implication of that. If God was His Father, then He was a being in God's class. That, to the Jews, was impossible. They held God in such towering esteem they could not speak out some of His names. You can imagine their amazement when Jesus dared to say, "God is My Father." If anybody was to make such a claim, it was not this particular young man. They knew His history.

A little over thirty years before, His 'father' and mother were engaged when the mother suddenly became pregnant. When the Jews asked her who did it, Mary insisted the Holy Spirit did. As if that was not the height of blasphemy, Joseph the carpenter, her suitor, concurred that the Holy Spirit actually made his betrothed wife pregnant. Now, who had heard such a thing! Of course, the Jews could not be convinced; they smelt a conspiracy. Joseph nonetheless went ahead and married Mary.

After some time the story died down. But some thirty years later the story resurfaced. This time, it was not the parents talking; it was the *man* born to them. He said God was His Father! To the Jews, who from His birth had viewed Jesus with guarded eyes, "This was extreme blasphemy!" That is why they took up stones to kill Jesus, as it were, to rid themselves of *the impostor*. Agreeing that God was His Father was equivalent to agreeing that He was a being on the same level as God.

You are gods

So Jesus asked why they wanted to stone Him, and they replied it was because He, being a man, was making Himself God. In response to that;

> **Jesus answered them, "Is it not written in your law, 'I said, "You are gods"'? If He called them gods, to whom the word of God came (and the Scripture cannot be broken), do you say of Him whom the Father sanctified and sent into the world, 'You are blaspheming,' because I said, 'I am the Son of God'?"** [9]

You see, "You are gods," which had always been there in the scriptures, the very scriptures those people believed in so zealously. Addressing some people in the past, Almighty God had said,

I said "You are gods and all of you are children of the Most High." [10]

I know these statements raise a lot of questions in the mind, but the argument follows simple logic that 'kind gives birth to kind.' Rather than worry about the sentiments evoked by these statements, let us consider the impact on our self-esteem. You cannot be the son of God and have a different nature. You must carry the God-nature. Come to think of it, God created man in His own image. This knowledge revolutionized my thinking. The question therefore is; "Do you have the nature of God?" "Should a god write an examination and fail? No way!" The knowledge that you have of God's nature removes limitations from your thinking!

Imagine a broke god!
Should a god be broke? Should a god beg for food? These are important questions. The nature of God puts Him beyond human limitations. His nature in us should also increase our capacity beyond human limits.

So, let's explore how having God's nature impacts on your capacity for success. The foundation for success is not what you have achieved or acquired, it is in who you are at the core of your being. Do you see yourself as a success, or as a failure? One of the greatest mistakes you can make in life is to use your circumstances or past performance to assess who you are. That is not who you are. That is what you have done. You are not what other people have said you are. You are who God says you are. You have the nature of God; therefore, walk upright with confidence! Walk tall! You are not just any other person walking on the street. You are unique. Whatever knocks others down should not knock you down. Likewise, you should not speak the way others speak. God does not speak like a beggar. You are not a failure trying to succeed; you are a success trying to give expression to your destiny. You are not a poor person struggling to become rich; your thought process must change the day God's nature comes into you. It all begins the day you ask God for forgiveness because Jesus already paid for mankind's sins.

With the nature of God, you are not a poor person struggling on the earth. You are a rich person trying to process your wealth from your heart into the material world! This was the discovery that changed my life. My success is not tied to the size of my car. My success is not tied to the amount in my bank account. Anything you see outside of me is only a reflection of what has happened inside me.

From *broke* to a millionaire
Some are waiting till they get millions in cash before they believe they are millionaires. That may take a long time. If you are a child of God you are already one. Poverty and disease came into our world as consequences of sin. Jesus paid for sin and its consequences. Can you now see where the mistake has been for a long time? The truth is that in God's estimation, you are rich. When you believe that, you become a success on the inside. Then you will attract and achieve equivalent success on the outside. When you become a millionaire inside, the millions have no choice but to find their way into your account, because, "as he thinks in his heart, so is he." And like Christ told His audience, "**the scriptures cannot be broken.**"

2
BATTLE
OF
IDENTITY

**Beloved, I pray that you may prosper in all things
and be in health, just as your soul prospers.** [1]

The soul of a rich person is different from the soul of a poor person. That is one of the revelations that changed my life. This is where the word 'self-image' is derived from. Self-image is the inner picture you have of yourself. From self-image we branch to 'self-esteem', which is how you feel about yourself. Then we branch to 'self-respect', which describes how you treat yourself. From self-esteem we gain 'self-worth'. Worth equals value. What do you think you are worth? That big question comes from how you picture yourself.

Your self-respect is displayed in how much you believe you are worth. There are people who treat themselves with respect and others who do not. Some people see themselves as common people or low class people, because they do not believe they have any value. It shows in their appearance, speech and conduct. They feel victimized by life's circumstances and envy the fortune of others. Your self-image will always control your behavior. You will never attempt to get anything beyond the limits that you set for yourself. If you change that inner picture that you have of yourself, you change your quality of life.

Refuse inferiority

In the beginning of man as the Bible tells it, Satan tempted Eve into believing that she would become as wise as God if she ate the forbidden fruit. Have you ever wondered why that one fruit was so important when there were so many she could choose and eat from with no consequences? The big deal was in the idea that she would become like God. It was the excitement of becoming like God that pushed Adam and Eve to eat the fruit. They were deceived because they were already created in the image of God. This was the first battle the enemy fought against the first man and woman; a battle he cunningly won. Satan made them to doubt that they were who God said they were. It is this same battle the devil confronts us with today. All he needs do is try to get you to believe that you are less than the person you already are. For Adam and Eve, God had said:

> **"Let Us make man in Our image, according to Our likeness…" So God created man in His own image; in the image of God He created him; male and female He created them.** [2]

How I love that! It means you have no excuse. Both men and women are included. God created us in His image and likeness but the devil pretends not to know that. "No!" He insists, "you can't just take it like that; your circumstances are proof you are not successful." The striking revelation here is, it was in the bid to become what they were already that Adam and Eve crashed. Are you struggling to become successful when God has declared you a success already?

The victory of the last Adam

Jesus Christ is referred to as the last Adam in the Bible. That means that if He failed, mankind would be doomed forever. When Jesus was baptized at River Jordan, the heavens opened and the Spirit of God descended on Him in the form of a dove. Then God spoke from heaven:

> **"This is My beloved Son, in whom I am well pleased"**[3]

After that, the devil came to tempt Jesus. His first salvo, as it is recorded, was:

> **"If You are the Son of God, command that these stones become bread"**[4]

The devil was implying that even though God called Jesus his son, that wasn't enough. Jesus needed to prove it. If Jesus turned the stone into bread, then He was the Son of God. If the stone did not turn into bread, then He was not the Son of God. Turning the stone into bread would have defined Jesus's success by performance. He would have fallen into the same trap that Adam and Eve fell into. Rather, Jesus replied:

> **"It is written, 'Man shall not live by bread alone, but by every word that proceeds from the mouth of God.'"**[5]

Jesus was saying, "Devil, I do not need to turn stones into bread before I realize who I am. My identity is not tied to my ability or actions. Whether I turn these stones into bread or not, I am who God says I am."

It is so powerful when your esteem is not built essentially on tangible things but on intangible truths and values. Please note that God said, *"This is My beloved Son, in Whom I am well pleased"* Jesus had not worked a single miracle at that point in his life. That was God declaring Jesus a success. Christ's success began from the inside out, not from the outside in.

Why wait for spectacular things?

Many of us use our achievements or non-achievements to define our level of success. That is a big mistake. You took an exam and failed; that is no reason to conclude that you are a failure. The devil notices the thought and amplifies it. But candidly, it was already designed into your destiny that you should be a success even before the examiner was born. And the day the nature of God came inside you, this became your reality. Natural parameters are too poor to measure what you are on the inside. There is a difference between failure as a person and failure at something. Stop trying to identify yourself by the things that have happened to you or by what you have. It is wrong to think that if you do not have money, you are poor. Do not build your self-esteem on material things.

On this earth, the raw material with which God builds is His word (or His idea). Whatever He calls a person or anything is what that person or thing becomes. You are who God says you are. The big question however is, do you believe it?

> **And this is the victory that has overcome the world, our faith**[6]

What you believe is what you become ultimately. God has created a powerful spiritual reality for you. Use it to change your physical circumstances. Let us take after Jesus's example when He boldly declared;

> **"The Spirit of the LORD is upon Me, because He has anointed Me to preach the gospel to the**

poor; He has sent Me to heal the broken hearted, to proclaim liberty to the captives and recovery of sight to the blind, to set at liberty those who are oppressed; to proclaim the acceptable year of the LORD." [7]

He believed this even before he began to perform miracles. Today, many people would not believe they are anointed or empowered unless they have raised someone from the dead or healed the blind. The problem is, you are not going to raise anybody from the dead if you don't believe you are anointed to do so. The anointing you do not believe in will not work for you. Such things start from the inside out. I call this scenario the battle of identity.

Stick with your God-nature

If you have God's nature in you, then you are not a failure; you are a success. Do not use your past experiences or status to define who you are. You are not defined by the struggles you have faced. More importantly, you are not what people say you are, because your destiny was planned before you were born. Unfortunately, some important people in our lives have repeatedly said some words that lodged deep in our hearts. We have unwisely allowed those words to control our lives. Perhaps you have been called a fool, or been told that you will never make it in life. Perhaps, some of the people who you let speak into your life have passed away and their words still control your life. No more!

Do not use lack of education to determine your value in life. Do not use the lack good appearances (we tend to feel inferior to people we feel have better self-presentation than we do) as a way to devalue yourself. You have as much as they have on the inside; the only difference is you are in the process of converting your inner success to its outer equivalent. Even if you had to walk to an event, and had to sit beside another person who came in a luxury car, you should not feel so embarrassed that you are unable to even say "Good Morning."

Take note, you may not have your luxury car today, but if you already drive one on the inside, it is only a matter of time before you get yours. Do not feel inferior. You are a person of value.

I have said that self-image will affect your behavior. There are stores and restaurants some of us have never visited, because we consider them to be too expensive. Why not visit these stores? Everything is created for you. Do not act based on your present outward circumstances; they are not the true reflection of who you are. Act on what God has said about you. You are a child of God. Every problem you come across is an opportunity for miracles, an opportunity for the power in your life to find expression. You are much bigger than the challenges you confront on the outside. You must believe before you become.

Express the new man in you

I can boldly declare that from today, you will attract opportunities you have never attracted before. Begin to dare things you have never thought possible because of your present qualifications. You have discovered now that if anyone was qualified on this earth for those opportunities, you are. If you see anything good around you today, tell yourself, "It's for me." Square up your shoulders; walk tall with a spring in your steps, because any moment from now what you say about yourself will happen. You are a miracle going somewhere to happen. You are the new arrival in town! One way you can stamp the image of your future look in your mind today is to take a picture of yourself in your best attire, make a big poster of it and write on it: COMING SOON!

All those who thought they knew you will very soon realize they never knew you at all. They see you in the process of evolution but they have not seen your finished state. Anybody who thinks that what they see on the outside today is your ultimate would discover very soon that they made a big mistake. Oh yes, you are in the process!

Time to live out your dream

People will only see you as you see yourself. If you do not see yourself as worth a lot, neither will anyone else. You deserve the best. Treat yourself well starting today. Walk into those stores you once thought were beyond your reach, and speak your breakthrough into existence. Imagine yourself owning the items you desire. You may even try out some items to get a better visualization. You will not get into trouble for doing this. It is a lack of self-image that stops people from going to places they believe is beyond their reach. These people are afraid. But you will not be arrested for not buying anything; such is your privilege as a customer. As it is said, the customer is king.

For instance, you have always wished to drive your dream car some day. Come on! Get on with it. Stop wishing. It is just about to happen. Go to the car dealership for a test drive. Check out a BMW, Lexus, Range Rover or Mercedes. Try out Jaguar or Audi. Experience what it is like to drive a Bentley and a Maserati. Ask them to see the cars, and open the doors. Sit down. Start the car. When you have made up your mind on the one you want, sit down to negotiate with the car salesman as if you have the money.

Let me share a secret with you. Money doesn't talk. No one knows how much anyone has. So, when you walk into the dealership, the car salesman does not know whether you have the money or not. You are the only one who can give yourself away. You do not even have to go in suit and tie, because rich people sometimes walk around in slacks and loafers. When you have real wealth, you do not have to try to prove anything to anybody. So act as if it is there, because it is right there in your heart! Negotiate with the car salesman. When you are through, tell the salesman, "I'll be back soon," because you are truly coming back soon. You are acting as if you have the money. You may not have it in your pocket yet, but you have it in your heart. Very soon it will move from your heart to your pocket, because "as he thinks in his heart, so is he."

3
PROGRAM YOURSELF FOR SUCCESS

You cannot break God's law

The point I have emphasized so far is that success must begin from the inside out. God's laws govern this world, and you cannot break them. You cannot change them. God invested tremendous energy in this world, energy that He put within the bounds of certain laws. When you satisfy the conditions of those laws, you generate tremendous force in your life to get things done. Respectively, when you break the conditions of those laws, they work against you.

When you operate within the law of sowing and reaping for example, there is nothing you can do to make a seed grow. Meet the conditions such as right season, humidity, temperature, and soil, and then plant your seed. There are sufficient nutrients in the soil already that will enter your seed and make it grow. If you want to live a successful life, tap into the power God has invested in nature. Use principles as a guide to achieve your goals.

You are what you say you are

Many of us have spent our lives defining ourselves by other people's definitions of us. Some of us have made the mistake of describing ourselves by what we have achieved in life. When we have money we believe we are rich; when we do not we believe we are poor. Be careful about 'I am' statements. When you talk to people, be conscious of the words: "You are a...." As you know, the words that hurt you greatly from other people are: "You are a... You are a fool or you are an idiot..." These words do not just criticize what you have done; they criticize who you are. That is why they hurt very deeply. Unfortunately, there are people who use negative labels on themselves. "Poor me, or Woe is me," they say. Well, you are not poor anymore!

Misleading titles

If your sense of success and achievement is tied to material possessions, titles or status then your self-esteem is low indeed. In some parts of the world, people are crazy about titles before their names. But if a person's name cannot stand on its own, the person is not worth his claims.

What you believe plays a role in what you become. If you believe that you are a success, begin to act like it. If you see God blessing anyone, it is a sign that yours is on the way. Ever noticed that successful people do not have two heads? If anybody is entitled to succeed in this world, you are entitled. Let me put it to you emphatically: You are intrinsically good. You are qualified for the best that God has to offer in this world. It is critical that you bear this in mind to change your status in life. Jesus begins a powerful statement:

> **"Either make the tree good and its fruit good, or else make the tree bad and its fruit bad; for a tree is known by its fruit."** [1]

All the things people call success and achievements are just fruit. Do you want good fruit? Stop focusing on the fruit alone. The fruit is a product of the tree. Until you change the tree you cannot change the fruit. What describes your nature is your character, from which we have the word 'characteristics'. Your character determines your future. I would like to emphasize that of all the success speeches you would ever hear in this world, if you do not hear the one that addresses your character, you have heard nothing. It is like trying to build a house from the roof. The foundation for success is your character.

Two levels of success

There is a difference between success as a person and success as an action. You took an exam and passed; that was an event. However, if we remove the passed exam, who are you? What is the state of your heart? Success is the achievement of goals. If your goal is to earn a hundred thousand dollars in sixty days, and you do this through fraudulent means, have you succeeded? Well, you achieved your goal, so you achieved success as an event. But as a person, you are a fraud.

Two standards of failure

There is also a difference between failure as a person and failure as an event. The problem we have today is that many people are confusing failure as an event with failure as a person. The fact that you failed an exam does not make you a failure. It was the exam that was a failure. I want to plead with you that from today- you do not internalize your failure. You are not what you have done and you are not what you have; you are who God says you are.

Setting moral goals

I have a message for the robber or fraudster. You may already have some qualities that make for success, but you lack character. Without character your success cannot last. You may have been able to plan, strategize and execute your plans and might I say that you have courage too since you take risks. There are indeed a lot of fearful people who do not venture into their dreams and end up achieving nothing. Unfortunately your goals are not moral. The same convictions that led you to do wrong can also lead you to do the right thing. There are people who have a peaceful mind and do not worry about the cops. I urge you to use your fantastic qualities to do the right things. Cross over to God's side, turn away from vice and evil. You can succeed with peace of mind.

That said, Jesus spoke clearly that you could not get good fruit from a bad tree. If it looks good, take caution because it could be rotten inside. When you allow God to change your nature (the tree), the fruit you bear will be good fruit. I found a critical formula for changing the state of your heart and ultimately your circumstances in this passage:

> **For the hearts of this people have grown dull. Their ears are hard of hearing, and their eyes they have closed, lest they should see with their eyes and hear with their ears, lest they should understand with their hearts and turn, so that I should heal them.** [2]

God says the reason these people are in their current situation is because something is wrong with their hearts. Their hearts are dull. A dull heart will result in a dull life. But I believe even now, that the power of the Holy Spirit will engage your heart and move you to a supernatural level. Your brain will begin to function on a new frequency. What is the key? The text says, "*Lest they should see with their eyes and hear with their ears, lest they should understand with their hearts.*" First the eye, then the ear, and then the heart. There are two gates to your heart: your eye-gate and your ear-gate. Whatever you see or hear consistently over a period of time will enter your heart. Whatever enters your heart has entered your life. The media industry runs on this principle, and it is successful at promoting to the eyes and ears.

The inner senses

You see things on two levels, because, really, you have two sets of eyes. You have both physical and spiritual eyes. You are designed with the capacity to relate with the spiritual world and the natural world at the same time. Both worlds affect your life. With your spiritual eyes you are able to see from the unseen realm. Understand that the basic components of spiritual communication are words and pictures. One immediate way to show this is through the way I am communicating to you in this book. The vehicle for communicating the ideas in my mind to you is simply by words. You can see it with your mind's eye as you read along. That is exactly how God communicates with you too. He throws words into your mind and sends you pictures. When you become conscious of those pictures and words, with time, you would be able to recognize which ones are from God and which ones are not.

There are many words that enter your mind daily; and with time you will be able to detect which ones are inspired from God. God is not human. So, do not expect to hear Him audibly under normal circumstances. You connect with Him through your thoughts. When you speak to God and are expecting Him to speak to you, clear your heart and mind. When His word comes to you, you will sense it in your mind and heart. It is typically different in effect from what human beings would say to you.

All Scripture is given by the inspiration of God[3].

When what He says comes to you, it will create a spontaneous idea and picture in your mind; you will know it was not the direct result of what you were thinking or saying. It will break through your current line of thought. You will know it is God because it would not be a product of your human mind. Generally, you can differentiate the ideas that come to you via your daily experiences from those that are uncommon.

Your inner eye needs to receive pictures from God. When you pray, expect God to show you pictures. When they come, keep those pictures protected and hold on to them. Once you sense they are from God, try to capture them by writing them down. The things God showed the prophets of old are the things written in the Bible, and you see the resulting miracles and breakthroughs because God inspired them. Write down the things you see in your heart. What is next? You must always take time to meditate on those things that God has said. Keep those things before your eyes. As with your inner eye, your inner ears can also hear things from heaven.

Creating beyond your environment

What you see with your physical eyes affects your heart and life. When you wake up every morning, what you see is crucial to your destiny because whatever you see consistently over a long period is what is stamped on your mind and heart. If the picture of the same room is stamped on your heart every day, you may remain there a long time. I am suggesting that you deliberately find a way of introducing better things for your eyes to see. In the Bible, God told Abraham to look up and count the stars, and that each star stood for his descendants. With that picture, Abraham broke through the barrier of barrenness. Even Jacob had to make spotted rods, which he put before his animals where they ate and mated. Those animals, though plain colored, were able to give birth to young ones with spots, just like the color of the wall placed before them.[4] It worked on animals. It works for humans. It is a law. What you see is what you become. I have applied this principle to different areas of my life because it is so powerful!

If you are looking through a magazine and there is anything in it that looks like where you are going in life, cut it out and stick it on the wall of your bedroom. Look at it every day. Just imagine if Abraham had responded with, "I need real children, not some starry images," When God told him to "look at the stars," he would definitely have missed his miracle. If your desire is a car, stick the picture of your desired car on the wall. If that car enters your heart, it enters your life.

The law of visual reality

My wife, Nike, and I once attended a conference where a speaker asked us to bring along the picture of the house we wanted. We went with the picture of a house. The interesting thing is that we cut it from the brochure of a car, with the car itself in front of the house. At the meeting, we were asked to lift our pictures for prayers, believing God to turn it into a reality. Since there was a car in the picture, we decided to ask God for the car and the house. We stuck that picture on the wall.

Sometime later, I went into a car dealership. I had momentarily forgotten the model of the car we had in the picture and had wanted to buy another one. "See, this other one is powerful," one of my friends who came with me said, pointing at a different car, "and there isn't much difference in their prices." I could see indeed that this other car looked powerful, but its shape did not quite justify its status, I thought. We asked the salesman to open up the car. I sat down in it, tested the buttons and immediately decided on it. When I got home, I told my wife that I was interested in buying a different car. I told her the brand of car I decided on. Then she said, "Yes, it's the one we've had in the picture on the wall." The point is, though I had momentarily forgotten the picture of the car we had on the wall, God made no mistake; the principle worked. That was the exact car I eventually bought.

But that was not the only car I would get like that. I have gotten several cars just by sticking the pictures on the wall and praying about them. Sometimes I do not have a picture. I write the type of car and its price on paper, and stick it there. On the wall in my bedroom there is always a check cut from my check book and addressed to me with a big amount drawn to me. I do that because I have discovered the law of visual reality works also in the area of finances.

Laws work irrespective of whom, where and when. If you want to fall down you do not need to say a prayer; simply climb up a story building and jump. God has already invested a force in life that will attract you to the ground. There is energy and power in the world to help you achieve your goals. Just surrender yourself to the principles of success.

My question to you now is: what do you see consistently? If you live in the slums, it is not a crime to start there, but do not hold on to such a place in your imagination. How do you move to the luxurious places in your city? You have to put pictures before your eyes. Occasionally, take a walk or drive round the beautiful parts of your city and stamp on your mind the picture of those delightful scenes.

Grab your season of promotion

Why am I sharing all these with you? It is because I believe this is the season of promotion for you. Your testimony is about to start wherever you are. All those who thought they knew you before are about to see a new person altogether. You see, some of us go through circumstances in life that make some people conclude that our situations cannot change. They really think they know us. They know where we came from, but it is not about where you came from, but where you are going. The only way your life will remain as it has been is if you keep looking backward.

Let me suggest to you that you visit your dream neighborhood. Walk through the streets. I did this once with my camera in Houston, Texas where I went visiting with a friend. I took pictures of the street. It was a new and clean community; and it had a man-made lake. It was such beautiful scenery. I have traveled with my family to countries more beautiful than ours, just so we could stamp pictures of excellence into our hearts to believe a new future.

Working wonders with mental creations

How do you create visual reality in your mind? Make a visit to that exclusive supermarket you cherish but have always avoided because you thought it was out of your price range. Dream. Put a new picture in your heart. Life does not give you what you deserve; it gives you what you are. Candidly, you deserve the best. However, you need to align with principles. Success is first within, and then without. Let me encourage you, therefore, that you begin to practice for the new level. Go where you have never gone before. Appear the way you have never appeared before. People's self-esteem is demonstrated by the way they carry themselves. There are people in their thirties or early forties who look like they are in their eighties, because they have given up on life. Yet, life should just be starting for them! Don't give up now, even if you are eighty. Get ready for a turn-around. Your tomorrow will be better than your yesterday!

SUCCESS IS WHAT YOU THINK

4

THINK AND SUCCEED

Thoughts are powerful. They can totally revolutionize your life. There is no force in this world that is strong enough to hold you down when you change your thoughts to fit God's plan for your life. Your thoughts are the seeds of all achievement. All material things began with a thought.

> By faith we understand that the worlds were framed by the word of God, so that the things which are seen were not made of things which are visible.[1]

The spiritual is superior to the material. The invisible is superior to the visible. The deceptive thing about the human nature is that it believes more in what it can see and feel physically. But the biblical verse above tells us that the raw materials God used to construct the material world were invisible.

The reality of invisible things

We are created in the image of God, and God is invisible. It is the invisible world that controls the physical world. In fact, to achieve any meaningful thing in this material world you must be a deal in the invisible. Everything in this material world is derived from thought. In the invisible world, thoughts are tangible things.

There is more to you than your physical body. When God created man, He formed his physical body from the soil. Then He released something into the body and man became a living soul. This gave man his two essential parts: the visible and the invisible. But you must put more value on your invisible part. That is the part of you that really impacts in this world. Your physical body is not worth much really. First, about sixty-five to ninety percent of it is water; the remaining percentage divides into few kilograms and mostly grams of calcium, potassium, phosphorus, magnesium, iron, and some other chemicals[3]. Are you surprised?

Your greatest value is not in your physical body. The part of you that really shakes things in this world is your spiritual part. But we cannot touch your spirit, can we? Even though we cannot touch it does not mean it does not exist. Invisible things are more real than material things. It was the invisible world that created the material one. God is more real than humans. He is the most powerful being in existence. Therefore, you must put more emphasis on the invisible dimension of your life.

Alter your thoughts

As stated earlier, in the invisible world, thoughts are tangible things. They are real things. So when you are able to relate with them in their invisible state, then you can exercise the ability God has given us as human beings to move them from their invisible state into the material state. In fact, one of the most powerful discoveries that man has made in this generation is that man can alter his life by altering his thought.

Developing parts of the world need a mental revolution. For a long time we have not placed much emphasis on thought. We have not seen it as a resource, which is why we call ourselves poor. We have preferred to be irrational. But, you see, for you to be able to do the will of God in your life, you need to change your thinking.

> **And do not be conformed to this world, but be transformed by the renewing of your mind, that you may prove what is that good and acceptable and perfect will of God.**[4]

I found out that there are a lot of people who do not understand their spiritual nature. They do not understand God and how He works. They want His miracles but they do not want to live by His principles. Yet, the miracles of God are rooted in His principles.

Quality of thoughts equals life

The only way your life will be different from what it is now is if you to change the way you think. The quality of your life will not be better than the quality of your thoughts. To change something in your life requires firstly renewing your mind. This is irrespective of whatever spiritual exercise you may choose to perform. Whether you choose to fast and pray or to go to church every day, it must result in the renewal of your mind. Simply stated, until your mind changes, your life is not going to change.

First, you must learn to challenge conventional thinking. Our minds are like a very fertile field. The problem with fertile soil is that even if you leave it without cultivation, something still grows on it. It may allow things to grow that you may not like such as weeds. We must therefore deliberately cultivate our minds.

Most people leave their minds open for other people and the society to dump their opinions in. With time they unwittingly inculcate and cultivate popular thinking patterns and culture and eventually produce the same results as everybody else. Refuse to conform to this world so you can rise above average. Align your thoughts with the word of God. When you do this, you will realize that you will be able to see miracles before they happen in your life. You step into success thinking. You cannot think like God and be a failure.

Beware of common sayings

A piece of advice: Decide to go in the opposite direction of the crowd with your thoughts as you press on towards God's will. If you do, you are likely to be right. That is one way to not be conformed to this world. For example, I challenge proverbs or common sayings that I consider limiting or pessimistic. They may sound philosophical but may be misleading. In fact, some are said to have come from the Bible. A very popular one is, "Heaven helps those who help themselves." Where does the Bible say that? Though it is implied, there is no direct statement like that. Here is another one: "Money is the root of all evil." Where is that in the Bible? The Bible actually says, "**The love of money** is a root of all kinds of evil." [5] We need to train our minds, to learn to challenge conventional thinking, and to conduct innovative thinking so we can be originators and not duplicators. Do not allow people to dump the wrong things in your mind.

There are general thought patterns about money that you must pull out of your mind so you can make progress financially. One idea is, "You use money to get money." That is only partly true. The root of all achievements is thought. You create wealth with ideas. Do not be stranded because you do not have money. If you act on the right ideas, you will get money. By the way, God did not use cash to create the world.

Recognizing opportunities

To 'recognize' simply means to see or encounter something familiar. If you flew into an airport and I was sent to pick you up and I had not met you previously or was not given a picture of you, it would be difficult for me to recognize you. There are a lot of opportunities flowing around us every day. Sadly, we do not recognize them because they have not been part of our dreams.

When I drive around cities, I see opportunities while others may see problems. If you have a problem-mentality, you will see problems everywhere. What some people call a "problem" is what others call an "opportunity". Yes, they are the same.

Problems and opportunities are one and the same. What you see depends on your mental training. You must deliberately cultivate thoughts of conscious success. The Bible tells us how to change our thinking, and that is the challenge I want to leave with you. The more you change your thoughts, the more you change your life.

Be not conformed to this world but be transformed by the renewing of your mind.[5]

The word 'transformed' in the scripture above is similar to the English word 'metamorphosis' which is the process of transformation. The development, especially of a butterfly, best describes the experience. It starts as an egg, and then becomes larva. From larva it becomes a caterpillar, and from caterpillar it becomes a butterfly. I have experienced this transformation, and it is a lifetime journey. As it changes from one stage to another, it undergoes a process of transformation.

Do not say, "Well, that is another option apart from prayer and fasting." No, they work together. You see, when you go into prayer, one thing you must come out with is a new dream and a new mindset. When you engage the Spirit of God in prayer, you see the situation the way God sees it. Before you prayed, all you saw was the problem; but having prayed, you receive help from God and are able to see the solution.

"Call to Me, and I will answer you, and show you great and mighty things, which you do not know." [6]

Spiritual problems versus material weapons

We must stop fighting spiritual problems with material weapons. We must stop trying to change situations that have an invisible root with visible weapons. The root of the negative situation you do not want is invisible. You cannot take visible weapons to deal with invisible things. "Though we walk in the flesh, we do not war according to the flesh. For the weapons of our warfare are not carnal but mighty in God for pulling down strongholds."[7]

We need to destroy some thought-patterns. The thought of failure is not an ordinary stronghold; it is a spiritual stronghold. The devil took time to program us for failure. Recognizing the source of the problem, you can cast down all negative imaginations or arguments *"and every high thing that exalts itself against the knowledge of God."* [8] Give no room to whatever thought that contradicts the word of God in your mind. Bring *"every thought into captivity to the obedience of Christ."*[9] You can hold thoughts captive. They are so powerful and can demobilize your life if you do not stop them. You can paralyze a thought. You can render a particular thinking pattern ineffective in your life. I pray that the kind of thinking that has kept some parts of the world in poverty will lose control over your mind. Amen.

The mind is the battleground, and it is the place where the devil really tries to influence our lives. The mind is the place where we succeed or fail. With God on our side, victory is assured.

5
PLANNING

Planning is organized thinking. It is the key to success. Lack of planning is the major reason for failure. Dr. Robert Schuller once said that, "most people fail not because they plan to fail but because they fail to plan."[1] When you have discovered the secret to building wealth, you will realize that the major key to making money is planning. If you want a million dollars but have no plan for getting it, you are only wishing for it, and may not get it. The key to the millions you seek is planning.

Sometimes, it is tough talking to people of faith about planning. Why? If you sit down and begin to calculate and write things down step by step, some wonder and ask, "Does that agree with faith?

Where is the place of miracles?" What they do not realize is that there is a powerful connection between faith and planning. Read this:

> I will stand my watch and set myself on the rampart, and watch to see what He will say to me, and what I will answer when I am corrected. Then the LORD answered me and said: "Write the vision and make it plain on tablets, that he may run who reads it. For the vision is yet for an appointed time; but at the end it will speak, and it will not lie. Though it tarries, wait for it, because it will surely come, it will not tarry. "Behold the proud, his soul is not upright in him; but the just shall live by his faith." [2]

This biblical passage is about faith, and it includes writing down your goals and plans. One major reason some people's faith does not have tangible achievement is the lack of a plan. Their visions are suspended in the invisible realm where their goals, visions and dreams do not have any opportunity of finding expression. You need a plan to turn your dreams to reality.

Why people do not plan

There are various reasons why people do not plan. I have already shown you one; if they are believers in God, they think there is a contradiction between faith and planning. A second reason is that some do not know how to plan. The third reason some people do not plan is they see it as too much trouble. They want the product but not the process. It is unfortunate that some people do not know that God thinks and plans. He is the Master Planner. There is no way you can live in this world and not know that it was planned in detail.

Setting realistic goals

While some people do not plan because it is too much trouble, others do not plan because they have experienced frustration from previously set unrealistic goals. But rather than give up on planning or goal setting, the answer lies in changing your style. Learn the principles. I have made unrealistic plans before too and I have learnt from my failures. For example, I was unemployed when I heard of a conference in South Korea. I set a goal that I was going to attend that conference that year. You can imagine how much it would cost to go to South Korea from Nigeria. At that time, the return ticket cost forty-two times the monthly salary of a graduate. Needless to say, I did not get close to the airport in Nigeria, much less South Korea. I got nothing. That goal was simply unrealistic.

Sometimes when people try to attain things like that and fail, they give up. But you need to realize that failure can be a learning experience. If you try and it does not work, you have at least discovered one way it does not work. Another reason some people do not plan is because of the promised 'Rapture' - the imminent catching away of true children of God at Christ's second coming. Since they will be on their way to heaven any time soon, they leave off any plan for the future.

A bag full of wrong notions

In the days of Paul the Apostle, believers thought Jesus would come in their time, much like we do today. Some of them had even stopped working because they were expecting Jesus. Paul had to warn them, *"If anyone will not work, neither shall he eat"* [3] I believe that Jesus Christ can indeed come any moment from now. But from the way Christ spoke of future events, He did not mean for people to suspend their lives here on earth while awaiting His coming. He said,

"Two women will be grinding at the mill: one will be taken and the other left." [4]

Jesus expects us to be working, as life will have to go on. He added, *"Then two men will be in the field: one will be taken…."* [5] He did not say we would all be lying down on the bed, idling away, waiting. You do not have to suspend your life. Live ready for Heaven at anytime; but do so while you continue your life here.

A life without plan

A life without a plan is contrary to all laws. When you break laws, they break you. When you work very hard without a plan, you lose direction like a ship on the high sea without a compass. A plan defines your destination and direction in life. There is a saying;

If the axe is dull,
And one does not sharpen the edge,
Then he must use more strength;
But wisdom brings success. [6]

In other words, the use of your mind will help give you direction. It continues,

The labor of fools wearies them,
For they do not even know how to go to the city! [7]

Before I give out a list of steps to planning, let me give one advice from what Jesus said. Plan your life like a military commander that is out to win a war, because there is an enemy against you. It is not necessarily the size of the army that wins a war; it is usually the superiority of strategy. Careful planning guarantees victory, because wisdom is better than might. Jesus raises a vital question in this statement:

> **"For which of you, intending to build a tower, does not sit down first and count the cost... Or what king, going to make war against another king, does not sit down first and consider whether he is able with ten thousand to meet him that comes against him with twenty thousand?"** [8]

God's winning strategy

Most of what we hear about spiritual warfare is prayer and fasting, which are very important. However, in the passage quoted above, Jesus emphasized strategy. He said you have to sit down first and consult. See if you will be able to achieve your goal with the resources at your disposal. You must pray and plan. You need to develop the ability to master details, and the ability to write things down and calculate. You do not make much progress in life if you do not have mastery of details. If in the past week you do not have on record how you spent your money, it may be part of the reasons you are not making a lot of it. You must have a plan. It is not just enough to say, "Next year, I'll achieve this or that."

The big question is, how? You must sit down to hash out a strategy. While praying to God, get ready for a revelation because God gives us winning strategies.

Specifics of planning

Step One

Decide on what you want. The starting point for planning is decision. If you have a revelation from God, that is the starting point. Decide exactly what it is you want to achieve. It may be getting a new job, starting a business, taking a course getting married or making your first million." Whatever it is, decide on a definite goal.

Step Two

Give it a deadline. Nothing becomes dynamic until it becomes specific. As long as you are vague, unstable and unsure of exactly what it is you want, or exactly when you want to get it, you do not get it. Life seems to cooperate with the person whose mind is made up. So decide on what it is, and decide on a deadline.

Step Three

Write down your goals. Every week I have goals written down, and the result is visible; I live a fulfilled life. Without goals, success is impossible. Can you imagine a football game if there are no end zones? You may be the world's best player; if there are no end zones, you cannot score a touchdown. Your game will be a frustrating. You can readily tell the score before the game begins. There will be no winner. Without clearly defined goals, life will be frustrating, and you may never discover the secrets of happiness. Outside of goals and definite plans to achieve them, you hardly experience fulfillment. Write down your short-term, medium-term and long-term goals.

Step Four

Develop a detailed plan for the achievement of your goal. You may not hit it dead on target always; sometimes you achieve more than you have written down, and at other times you achieve a little less. But the plain truth is, once you have a detailed plan set out ahead of time, there is a force that takes you from where you are towards your set goal.

Let me make it very simple. How do you raise ten thousand dollars for your business? If you can have ten people who can give you a thousand dollars each, you have your ten thousand. If you could get twenty people to give you five hundred dollars each, you have your required capital. If you could get a hundred people to give you a hundred dollars each, you have the deed done. You can revise the plan and pick some of ten, some of five, some of one till you make up the full sum. More importantly, you are praying while you are doing that. Usually, while you are listing the sources you know, the Holy Spirit will nudge you on which options to explore and which not to explore. If your ideas are not enough to achieve the objective, the Holy Spirit gives you winning ideas. He does not want you begging where He has not put your blessing.

When God blesses you, He makes you rich without putting you to shame. As a Proverb says, *"The blessing of the LORD makes one rich, and he adds no sorrow with it."* [9] He blesses us with honor and dignity.

Step Five

Decide the services and product you will give in exchange for what you want. That is very important. You do not get something for nothing.

You do not focus on being a go-getter; focus on being a go-giver. When you give you will get. Decide what to give to get what you want. If you do not have the required skill to match your expected level of success, decide how to acquire that skill. Attend a course or become an apprentice somewhere.

Step Six

Dream about your goals every day. Keep those pictures at the top of your mind. See your dream as a miracle that has happened, in your mind.

SUCCESS
IS WHAT
YOU SEE

6
INSIGHT

What you see is what you will become. The word of God is described as a mirror in which we behold the glory of God and are changed into His image from one level of glory to the other. Let me put it another way. What you see in the word of God is what you will become in the world. This is a critical key to transformation.

Your two sets of eyes

All human beings have two sets of eyes: the physical eyes by which you see the material world, and your inner eyes, which are critical to your success in this life. You cannot see the glory of God with your physical eyes. God is a spirit, and you can only relate with, sense or perceive Him by your inner man.

The power of insight

What makes the difference between successful people and failures is the word *insight,* which, if you break it up, is a combination of two words: 'in' and 'sight'. Sight is the ability to see. With 'in-sight', you have the power to see things from the inside. It is about the operation of your inner eye. All of us see but we perceive differently. That is what makes the difference. What a failure calls a problem, the successful person sees as an opportunity. What the poor person calls a problem, the rich sees as opportunity for making money. It is all about what you see, and how you see.

Insight is very critical to our success in life. If someone's physical eyes are functioning but his inner eyes are blind, there is no combination of opportunities that will make him a complete success. On the other hand, a person's physical eyes are blind but the inner eyes are open, the person still has all chances of fulfilling their destiny. Our success depends a whole lot more on what we see with our inner eyes than what we see with our physical eyes. In fact, it is what you see with your inner eyes today that you will see with your physical eyes tomorrow. What you see is what you become.

You must have eyes that recognize opportunities. There is nobody in the world that lacks opportunities to succeed. We only have people who do not recognize their opportunities.

> **That the God of our Lord Jesus Christ, the Father of glory, may give to you the spirit of wisdom and revelation in the knowledge of Him, the eyes of your understanding being enlightened…**[1]

Now, think about the word 'understanding'. The invisible part of a building is what holds up the visible one. There is something under what is standing. It is the invisible world that created and controls this natural world. The physical building you see has a foundation that you cannot see. That simply illustrates the relationship between the visible world and the invisible world. The eyes that see beyond the natural are the eyes of your understanding. It is your inner eyes that perceive the causes of the things that are happening in the natural dimension.

Having your understanding enlightened is like having the light turned on. You recognize things you were not aware of before. It helps you to define your target or your destiny in life, and to know what to do to produce specific results. It helps you to discover new dimensions to yourself. At anytime, your potential is greater than your circumstances.

The role of the Holy Spirit

> **But this is what was spoken by the prophet Joel: 'And it shall come to pass in the last days, says God, that I will pour out of my Spirit on all flesh; your sons and your daughters shall prophesy, your young men shall see visions, your old men shall dream dreams.'** [2]

When you are filled with the Spirit of God, He activates your inner faculty. He opens your inner eyes and ears. You are then able to relate with the invisible realm. By the way, God made the law that controls life: If you can see things on the inside, you would see them on the outside.

And the Lord said to Abram, after Lot had
separated from him: "Lift your eyes now and
look from the place where you are: northward,
southward, eastward, and westward; for all
the land which you see I give to you and your
descendants forever."[3]

You see, it is not enough for God to see the good things He has
prepared for you. You must see the future yourself. Before you were
born, God already saw good things concerning you. But the way
this principle works, you have to see things for yourself. You have
to take control of your future by cooperating with the Holy Spirit
to dream about tomorrow. You can see beyond your present reality.
You can see the future before it arrives. If you see it, you will get it.

Why some people cannot see

We are told that some people are prevented from using their inner
eyes.

Whose minds the god of this age has blinded,
who do not believe, lest the light of the gospel
of the glory of Christ, who is the image of God,
should shine on them. [4]

This is how the devil works. If he is going to prevent a person from
moving into a new level of success, he blinds them. If they do not
see success with their inner eyes, they cannot enjoy it in real life.

Then Jesus lifted up His eyes, and seeing a great
multitude coming toward Him, He said to Philip,

"Where shall we buy bread, that these may eat?"
But this He said to test him, for He Himself knew
what He would do. Philip answered Him, "Two
hundred denarii worth of bread is not sufficient
for them, that every one of them may have a
little." [5]

Jesus asked Philip, "Where will we get bread for these people to
eat?" It was a test. He wanted to see how far Philip had come in his
training. Philip's brain was tied to the amount of money available.
They could only afford to give each person a small ration of bread,
and even at that, the bread would not go round.

The danger of scarcity mentality

Scarcity is not a problem. Scarcity mentality is the real problem.
What I do not have in my pocket right now, I can have in my heart.
If I have it in my heart, I am going to have it in my pocket, because
"as he thinks in his heart, so is he."

When Jesus asked Philip where they could get bread to feed the
crowd, Philip experienced a brain-block. He is not alone. Most
of us experience a brain-block when confronted with projects or
situations that require resources we do not have. The two hundred
denarii[7] Philip spoke about were the 200-day wage or salary for
the average worker at a denarius per day. This is the problem with
those who earn salaries and cannot see beyond the limitations of
their monthly pay. What you see with your physical eyes gets to
enter your inner eyes if you look at it long enough. When you keep
looking at your salary, after some time, your thinking becomes
confined to only what that salary can do.

But your salary is just one of your streams of income. *"My God shall supply all your need according to His riches...."* [6]

The moment you allow 'scarcity' to enter your mentality, you are broke! Please break free from a lack mentality. You may experience lack in the material world, but you must continue to live in the world of abundance in your heart. Amazingly, when Jesus tested Philip; the Bible says, *"He Himself knew what He would do."* In other words, Jesus already saw the crowd fed. Eventually, He fed them, without the money. ***What you see inside today, you will see outside tomorrow.***

Dispel your fears and confusion

Break free from confusion and anxiety. If you do not have a job, it is a temporary situation. If you have seen the glorious future ahead, you cannot be frustrated in the present. You will not be unemployed forever. You might as well enjoy your life now. By the time the job comes, you may not have enough time to read books or to do many of the things you have time to do now. You are on pre-job break. Therefore, get excited! Things are not as bad as they seem. Any moment from now, things are going to turn around for you.

7
IMAGINATION

An amazing truth unfolds to us in an ancient story where the prehistoric people got together and decided to build a city whose tower would reach up to heaven. When God saw what they wanted to build, He admitted that those people could not be stopped from doing what they had imagined or purposed.[1] In proposing or planning their project, those people engaged the forces of their imagination. Surprisingly, God said they would have whatever they had imagined to do though their project was against God's plan. That is how powerful the principles that control our world are. They work once their conditions are satisfied, not minding who is involved or the nobility of their intentions.

Your picture determines your future

To stop the building of the tower, God confused the speech of those people. They began to speak different languages. It was not really their language that He was after; it was the picture in their hearts. As long as that picture could be sustained, it was going to happen. God had to disable that picture. The moment they could not understand themselves anymore, the picture began to reduce in size until it eventually disintegrated. That was the only way to stop the project.

Imagination turns impulsive thoughts or ideas into pictures in the mind. When God designed you, He put in your mind that equipment that turns impulses and thoughts into pictures. *Imagination is simply image formation.* Our imagination functions like the film in a camera or like a memory card. When you have an image on the film or card, you can print it on a postcard. It is the image on the film that is printed out for you on the post card.

Whatever picture stays on the film of your mind or in your memory long enough will eventually be printed out for you in real life. One of the reasons people live frustrated lives is because they expect God to change their circumstances when they have not changed the image on their film. They expect the picture on the outside to change without first changing the picture in their imagination. God *"is able to do exceedingly abundantly above all that we ask or think..."*[2] The prayers of many are not answered because what they are asking for does not agree with what they are thinking. When you pray, and the power of God comes on your life, whatever image it meets on the film of your heart is what it prints out for you in real life. That takes us back again to the basic principle: *the quality of your life cannot be better than the quality of your thoughts.* It is your picture that determines your future.

Making grand change God's way

When God wants to change people's lives, He first changes their imagination. If the film in your heart is negative, God will not work against His principles to create favorable circumstances for you. He does not break His principles.

God promised to give Abraham a child but inside the mind of Abraham had been stamped a picture of barrenness. He even said it to God: "You said You will give me descendants, yet I am childless." God told him to step out of his tent and count the stars. Of course, he must have been unable to count all the stars. Then God said; "As many as those stars are so would your descendants be." ³ God was stamping a picture on Abraham's heart and mind.

God wanted Abraham to see more than just stars, because He wanted to break the barrier in Abraham's mind. God wanted to take him from a scarcity mentality to an abundance mentality. "Each star stands for your children," God told him. So every night when Abraham looked up, he saw stars. Each star probably turned into the face of a child crying out to him. Some may have called him "Grandpa" as he looked into the sky. Who knows? Later on in the story, God went a step further. He changed the names of Abram and Sarai and they became Abraham and Sarah.⁴

The interesting thing here is Abraham was 99 years old and had lost the natural capability to father a child. Sarah also was well past menopause. Naturally speaking, she could not have a child anymore. Usually at that age, the gait is gone; the delicate steps of a prime lady are all gone and all the vital statistics are no longer vital. As far as Sarah was concerned, she was past her prime! Yet God gave her a new vision.

The impact of a transformed mind

Every married man knows that what you say to your wife really matters. You can create big problems through what you say to her. Conversely, you can bring a new radiance to her face when you call her 'Princess'. When you tell your wife, "You are too fat," you hurt her self-esteem. For the next one hundred days, she would be looking at the mirror wishing for changes. What you have said, in fact, stamps a stronger picture on her mind and emotion than the reality of her looks. God taught Abraham to address her the other way: "Call her Princess." Though old and out of shape enough to know it, Sarah began immediately to radiate a new charm. Because what her husband said was now making a stronger impression on her mind and emotion than the reality.

Before long, Sarah brought out her chest of cosmetics and began those delicate touches on her skin all over again. She pulled out her discarded skirts and blouses; the dashing gait and exuberance of youth came back. Sarah was calling her husband Abraham: father of many nations. Gradually, those fitting words began to strike the right chords and stamp the new pictures on their minds and hearts. Of course, they must have sounded very ridiculous to everybody else in town. Imagine the old couple: Abraham, 99 years old, calling his 89-year-old wife 'Sweet Sixteen'! Obviously, the younger people in town must have thought those old folks were out of their minds. But no, the couple thought differently because they were getting ready for a miracle. *What you see inside today is what you will see outside tomorrow.* God would have a big problem creating your tomorrow if He cannot stamp it in your imagination now.

Abraham and Sarah later went down to Gerar where the king almost added her to his harem of wives.[5] What was a king who had access to all the beautiful virgins in town looking for in an 89-year-old woman? Sarah was not looking 89 anymore; her body was changing into the picture in her imagination. She was becoming so attractive that even a king wanted her. She eventually gave birth to Isaac.[6] *If God can change your imagination, He will change your life.*

The exciting world of imagination

Imagination is powerful. The snag is our natural circumstances, like lack of material things, tend to stamp an impression that is too strong on our imagination. If God does not remove those pictures off our minds and stamp a superior one on us through the revelation and power of the Holy Spirit, it becomes very difficult for us to accept what God says as a greater reality than what our circumstances say. God says:

Call to Me, and I will answer you, and show you great and mighty things, which you do not know.[7]

There is a new level for you, but you have to see it with your inner eyes. Your imagination is an asset to you; do not waste it. It is only in your imagination that you cannot be limited by time or space. Physically speaking, I can only exist at a point in time. But in my imagination I can live in the past, and I can live in the future. Through the power of imagination, I can join Moses at the crossing of the Red sea and see how God delivers 'us' from Pharaoh in Egypt. Living in the past is possible in my imagination.

I can live in the future too: a time when you could drive a car and by pushing a button, the car would take-off into the air. It is more than a James Bond movie and will be a reality. You wonder how that can be. Just what do you presume it means when God says man should have dominion over the fish of the sea, over the fowl of the air and over every creeping thing that moves on the earth? Your physical body cannot accomplish all that, because it is limited by time and space. There is a limit to how much weight you can carry with your hand. The part of you that really carries things, achieves big things and moves things on this earth is your invisible part. The major part of it depends on your imagination.

Break the limits of time. Break the limits of space. You can only be in one place per time. For instance, if you decide to travel to the United States from say, Nigeria, it will take you at least 12 hours if you fly non-stop, but in your imagination you can be there in split seconds, driving into the White House unimpeded to eat breakfast with the President of the United States of America. Is that not wonderful and exciting! The imagination is where you can really exercise your dominion. That is where you can break free from the limitations of your current circumstances. It does not cost you anything to dream. So I want to urge you: If you do not want your today to be repeated tomorrow, do not allow your current circumstances to enter your imagination. Present your imagination as a slate to the Holy Spirit. Let Him paint the picture of a better tomorrow on your heart at the place of prayer. You may be feeding on low profile meals on the outside today, but in your imagination you are on the fast track, feeding on a seven-course meal. You may be putting on used clothing and eating out in backstreet eateries today but do not let your low state of affairs rule your imagination. In your imagination, see yourself in a five-star hotel in a tuxedo, about to have dinner with a Prime Minister or President. Well, not everyone will get to do that, but focus your imagination on God's great plans for your life. I challenge you to break through your current limitations.

The miracle of Pentecost[8]

In the ancient story earlier mentioned, God had confused the language of mankind to destroy the picture in their mind. Something remarkable happened at Pentecost; God fused man's languages into one. While each of the Disciples of Christ spoke in tongues (a language they did not understand), some of the onlookers from Iraq listened and heard the disciples speak in Arabic. The person who came from Europe heard the disciples speaking French; another heard German, another, English. Some other person heard them speak Hebrew, while some others heard Greek. But this happened as different people listened to the same person. Now, something tells me that if God confused man's language to destroy the picture in the heart of man, when He unified human languages, He restored the power to dream. No wonder Peter said;

> "But this is what was spoken by the prophet Joel:
> 'And it shall come to pass in the last days, says
> God, that I will pour out of My Spirit on all flesh;
> your sons and your daughters shall prophesy, your
> young men shall see visions, your old men shall
> dream dreams.'" [9]

When you are baptized in the Holy Spirit, your capacity to dream is restored to you. As you read this and pray, I trust God that every limitation and barrier in your life will be shattered, regardless of how long those circumstances may have existed. You may be broke but you will not be broke in your spirit anymore. The Holy Spirit will paint the picture of abundance on your spirit.

The language of the Holy Spirit is the language of visions and dreams. Do not wait until you fall into a trance to see things. The Holy Spirit will paint pictures in your imagination while you are praying. When I pray I see things. Somewhere along the line, I find myself in real life in just the same situations that I saw while praying. And I find this very exciting and that is why I can talk about it. Today, I find myself in certain situations and wonder: "This was once a dream. Now it is a reality. This was the person I dreamt I was going to be." Dreams do come to pass.

I prophesy on everyone reading this book that every blind spiritual eye be opened. In no distant future, there will be a clear picture of the solution to what has been a problem. The vision that will establish your promotion will be stamped on your heart. Pictures of failure, of disappointments and frustrations, of lack and barrenness, are declared destroyed. Receive a miracle in your imagination. What you would see, like Abraham saw, will last beyond your lifetime. You will leave it as a legacy and inheritance for your children and your grandchildren. From here on, the curse of failure is broken. Poverty is broken, shattered and destroyed; it will not be found in your family lineage anymore.

The power of God will engage your life and begin to turn your dreams into reality. As you move out each day, may you come into opportunities and encounter miracles. Doors of favor will open for you. There will be supernatural acceleration in your life, and things will happen faster than you expect.

8
DREAM

I n this world, we owe all progress to practical dreamers. Thomas Edison, the famous inventor, dreamt that a bulb that would produce light by electricity. It was a dream, which has long become a reality as we know it. The Wright Brothers had a dream to fly. Their dream did not look possible, but in their minds, it was true and real. Today, millions of people are transported every year across the world in airplanes. I do not know if the Wright Brothers themselves had imagined that we would one day have jumbo jets, as tall as buildings, and as heavy; yet able to fly through the sky with hundreds of people across thousands of miles.

Guglielmo Marconi dreamt of the intangible forces of the chemical called *ether*. He believed that it would one day be possible for human beings to communicate across long distances without cables or wires. His friends thought he had gone nuts. He sounded absolutely unrealistic. Today, we are enjoying the reality of his dream. Henry Ford also had a dream of producing engines that ran by combustion. He believed that every family in America should be able to afford a car. That was once a dream. He started on this experiment in a garage. Today, the average household in the United States owns a car.

I do not know if it is still being said, but there was a time when people used to say, "See Paris and die," because of its beauty. Some people saw it, designed it and built it. We owe all the progress we see to practical dreamers because this world only gets better in people's dreams. So I want to urge you to dream, because *your dreams today are the raw material which God will use to create your tomorrow. If you do not have a dream, you do not have a future!*

The certainty of a dream

I have discovered that the people who became great in Biblical times were people who received dreams from God. Abraham was a dreamer. Jesus made a statement about him,

> **"Your father Abraham rejoiced to see my day, and he saw it and was glad." Then the Jews said to Him, "You are not yet fifty years old, and have you seen Abraham?"** [1]

The Jews could not imagine that Abraham who died a long time before Jesus was born could have seen Him. Abraham saw Jesus before He was born. The coming of Jesus was not just an apparition or merely wishful thinking; it was something Abraham knew would come to pass through his lineage. So, he could begin his excitement from that moment onward because it was impossible for it not to come to pass. It was God who gave him the dream.

Two levels of dreams

You can dream on two levels. You can dream on the natural plain, which is the first level. You can design a dream for yourself. You can advertise your future to yourself, because even God used natural things to stamp pictures on people's minds in the Bible. So, if you have a future that you desire and can get a picture of it, place it on the wall where you can see it often.

However, there is a second level - a supernatural dimension where God Almighty who cannot lie paints a picture in your heart. This, of course, is superior, because God is not a man that He should lie, nor a son of man that He should change His mind. If He said it, He will do it. [2] That is the kind of revelation that Abraham got. He saw the future. If God has given you a dream about your future, you should be excited. Every negative situation you experience on the way is temporary because God has told you what will come to pass.

At the Lincoln Memorial March in Washington in 1963, Martin Luther King Jr. declared: "I have a dream." He had a dream that one day the children of former slave owners and the children of former slaves would be able to sit together. It has happened. It was once a dream.

Dream beyond your borders

You can break beyond the borders of your present limitations to create a new future. The Bible tells us about Jacob and his children, in particular about Joseph who was his second to last child. Jacob loved Joseph so much that he gave him a coat of many colors. Joseph's brothers were envious and hated him.

> **But when his brothers saw that their father loved him more than all his brothers, they hated him and could not speak peaceably to him. Now Joseph had a dream, and he told it to his brothers; and they hated him even more. So he said to them, "Please hear this dream which I have dreamed: There we were, binding sheaves in the field. Then behold, my sheaf arose and also stood upright; and indeed your sheaves stood all around and bowed down to my sheaf." And his brothers said to him, "Shall you indeed reign over us? Or shall you indeed have dominion over us?" So they hated him even more for his dreams and for his words. Then he dreamed still another dream …[3]**

Joseph's brothers insulted and verbally abused him. They dismissed him and made him feel like he would never amount to anything. But in the midst of all that Joseph had a dream. From Joseph's experience, we can see how important our responses are when we face the challenges of life. Most people give their challenges as excuses for failure. But God has put within you the capacity to overcome your current external circumstances with an internal circumstance. On the outside, Joseph was harassed and counted as nothing; he was dominated and intimidated by his older brothers. With his God-given dream, however, he was favored above them within the context of his purpose. On the outside, his brothers had authority over him but it was the other way round in his dream. The first place to overcome your challenges in life is in your dream. The first place to overcome poverty is in your dream. The first place to ride over joblessness is in your dream. I pray that God will give you a new dream.

Joseph told his brothers, "I had a dream and I saw all of you bowing down to me." Filled with envy and hate, the brothers wondered, "You?" They hated him even more for his dreams. How did Joseph respond to that? Verse nine says,

Then he dreamed still another dream...

The bigger the problem became, the bigger Joseph's dreams grew. He had seen eleven bundles of crop bowing down to his own bundle in the first dream. They hated him for that. So the next time he showed up, he claimed to have another dream where the sun, the moon, and the eleven stars bowed down to him. It was a bigger dream!

Victory through your dream

You were created in the image of God. Whatever is born of God overcomes the world.[4] The place where you first overcome the world and life's challenges is in your dream. How do you respond to the challenges of your life? You may not have food to eat now; yet the exciting thing is, you can eat anything you want in your imagination and dreams. A spiritual law affirms that *whatever you see on the inside is what you would see on the outside tomorrow.* We must be careful not to allow our current circumstances to create our future circumstances for us. If you do not deliberately prevent your outside from getting inside you, you will find yourself in a cycle. That is why it is important that while you are going through whatever you are going through today, you must have a new dream for tomorrow.

I think it is exciting to dream because it gives you temporary relief. I think when you are hungry you can switch over into your dreams and begin to imagine yourself in a five-star hotel having dinner. You can imagine yourself taking the first course, the second course, and then the third…. This may be hard, but when you do the hard part first, things tend to get easier.

When it was time for Joseph's dream to be fulfilled, his brothers sold him to slave-traders who took him to Egypt where, by divine providence, he later became prime minister. His brothers came to the land in search of food because of famine in the region. Later, when they returned again for food, Joseph startled them when he revealed that he was their 'lost' brother. By the time he said that, his brothers had already bowed a number of times to him, in fulfillment of the dream.[5]

Beware of the danger of sin

Whatever the obstacles, however difficult it may be in your environment, understand that *there is no peculiar situation that is strong enough to stop your God-given dreams from coming to pass.* Watch out for the person who wants to lure you into sin. Watch out for the person who wants you to take a bribe or to commit sexual sin. Watch out, because your dream is just a seed; and if an insect is introduced into it, it will eat the life out of your dream. The dream becomes an empty shell, having lost its life and possibility for growing into maturity. *You cannot succeed without character.*

Run away from sin. In the process of doing so, you may lose your coat as Joseph did with his boss' wife. While he escaped out of her hands, she held his coat as proof that he tried to rape her. Joseph lost his coat. It was the second coat he would lose. His brothers took his first coat of many colors, which his father gave him. If you stand for what is right, you may lose some coats. You may lose relationships, jobs and opportunities. But if the devil wants to steal your coat, let him steal it. Just do not let him steal your dream. When the dream eventually comes to pass you will be able to have better and as many coats as you please. *When your coat is lost nothing is lost. But when your character is lost, all is lost.*

The dawn of a new day

I believe sincerely in my heart that *this is the generation of the greatest dreamers the world has ever seen.* A few years down the line you will share testimonies, because you will be living in the reality of your dreams. Then we will tell the younger generations: "This was once a dream." I once dreamt of the day I would stand before thousands of people to speak. I even did some rehearsals before the mirror, speaking to nobody in the physical, except the people in my dream. Today, that dream is a reality. Your dreams are coming to pass!

SUCCESS
IS WHAT
YOU KNOW

9
INFORMATION

nformation is the key to transformation. The quality of your life cannot be better than the quality of information available to you. I therefore want to suggest that you place value on information.

> **The Spirit of the Lord GOD is upon Me, because the LORD has anointed Me to preach good tidings to the poor...**[1]

What is good news to a poor person other than that he can break free from poverty? Dr David Oyedepo once said, "to be informed is to be transformed and to be uninformed is to be deformed."

If you break 'information' into two parts, you would have 'in' and 'formation.' Formation in construction simply means to create in a shape. It therefore implies that information is the knowledge that shapes you internally. *It is your in-formation that determines your out-formation.*

Before information affects your circumstances, it will first affect your thinking. You will be transformed by the renewing of your mind. Knowledge simply changes you on the inside. If it can change you on the inside, then it can change you on the outside. Notice, that the major part of 'formation' is 'form', which means to construct, to make, to create, to shape. There is tremendous power in information. Let me use a scriptural illustration. It opens with Jesus saying,

> **"It is written, 'Man shall not live by bread alone, but by every word that proceeds from the mouth of God.'"** [2]

Here, information is compared to food, because what food is to your physical body is what information is to your soul. Your physical body grows, is renewed and sustained by what you eat and drink. That is exactly what information does to your spirit. I urge you to put emphasis on information. Make it a habit to learn something new every day. If you expect to live a better quality of life in the coming years, then you need to commit to learning.

Man's greatest enemy

God, speaking through prophet Hosea says, *"My people are destroyed for lack of knowledge."* [3] So man's greatest problem is ignorance, not the devil. The devil only thrives on human ignorance. Apostle Paul affirmed this.

Lest Satan should take advantage of us: for we are not ignorant of his devices.[4]

This means that Satan uses our ignorance to take advantage of us. The entrance of light is the disappearance of darkness; the Bible helps us understand that the devil and his minions are agents of darkness. They only operate in darkness, not in the light. Therefore, place value on information from the light so you can be free from oppression. It is the truth that sets you free.

He who despises the word will be destroyed, but he who fears the commandment will be rewarded.[5]

The person who despises information, this text says, will be destroyed; but the one that has respect for the commandment will be rewarded. My suggestion to you is that you spend time with the word of God. There is nothing you need: husband, wife, children, money, promotion, and breakthrough that is not in the word of God. If you can find what God has to say about it, He will help you find it in the world.

But we all, with unveiled face, beholding as in a mirror the glory of the Lord, are being transformed into the same image from glory to glory…[6]

What you see in the word is what you will become in the world. I prophesy on you that now, you will receive revelations.

Every time you open the Bible, God will open the Bible to you. God will bring across your way the books that contain the information that will take your marriage, career and business to a new level.

The most valuable place in my house is the study. I often come out from my study intoxicated with knowledge. In my library, I engage with others minds around the world through their books. Iron sharpens iron.[7] When people come across a successful person, what they look for is the secret to their success. They look for the wisdom, which is the root of the success the person is experiencing. Wisdom is the real deal. It empowers you to create new realities.

10
EDUCATION

Education is about formation

Education simply implies training your mind or inner faculties. It means to bring forth from within or to draw out. So, education trains and transforms you on the inside, and empowers you to design solutions for the problems that you meet in real life. Information never leaves you the same. It transforms you on the inside. It reconstructs you. It changes your capacity from the inside. It is your 'in' formation that determines your 'out' formation. That is the goal of education.

I was watching my kids some time ago playing games on the computer and I reflected back to when I was their age. If someone had said 'computer' back in my day, I would most probably have thought that was the name of an angel. I often think about how different the games my children play are from what I used to play was when I was their age. I realized that most children in third world countries play with material things, not things that challenge the mind. They naturally grow into adults who have learnt to relate only with material things, not mental processes or creative activity.

The two components of education

There is formal education, a vital part of the process of our transformation, which we should all take seriously. Developing countries need a revolution in their school curriculum. A system that encourages you to cram or memorize things for the purpose of passing examinations, after which you forget everything, is not education. The goal of education is not just information; it is formation. When you make people cram and do exams, all you have achieved is information. But when you train them to be able to use their minds to create, produce and design solutions to life's situations, then they are educated. Many people are literate but not educated. They have passed through university but they cannot design any products or services with which to resolve their circumstances. What is the solution? Let us build schools that will produce the citizens that will build a new nation.

The other form of education is the informal, which includes self-education. It involves reading other than for exams. In my case, for instance, I trained as an engineer but today I work in fields for which I was not initially trained in school. Today, that is the sort of thing we need, because education is not supposed to make you myopic; it is supposed to expand your horizon and help you to think. Once the foundation is laid with formal education, you have to build on it. Many stop studying the day they finish their last exam in school. Of course, the implication is that they stop growing in knowledge.

**A wise man will hear and increase learning, and
a man of understanding will attain wise counsel.**[1]

Buy the truth

I am pleading with you that you put value on information. Buy books. *If you want an outcome you have never had before, read something you have never read before.* Increase your information. Solomon, the wise king, said; *"Buy the truth, and do not sell it."*[2] Investment is the key to achievement. Buy books and read them. Your success in life is tied to your thinking. *If you do not have time to think you do not have time to succeed.* Increase the quality of your thoughts.

Your challenges are not unique; somebody experienced something similar fifty years ago and wrote a book containing the solution. Why should you now go through the same stress? Experience is the best teacher, as long as it is not your own experience. You do not have enough time in your life to go through all the problems other people have gone through. Take a short cut. Accelerate your own journey. Start from where they stopped. Read their books.

Pay attention to your mental development. Take a course; read; attend seminars; and listen to CDs. God Himself says;

"Come now, and let us reason together…"[3]

Unfortunately, the only thing people do when they go to God is talk. They do not like to do strategic thinking. But, "let us reason together," God says. You cannot relate with God and insist you will not use your mind. He wants to take you to a higher dimension of thinking. I pray that God brings your way good books that will change your status.

11
REVELATION

We access information on two dimensions. There is the natural and there is the supernatural. The natural dimension of information is acquired through our five senses. However, it is now an established fact that there is more to our world than our five senses can relate with. The supernatural dimension of information is acquired through our intuition.

To reveal means to unveil or to bring into the open what has been hidden. God created and influences our world through the power of revelation. When He introduces His thoughts into the human mind, it literally causes a revolution.

For one, God's perspectives to issues are on a higher dimension than ours. It is like the difference in perspectives between someone walking on the ground and someone flying forty thousand feet above sea level. What is an obstacle to the man on the ground does not exist to the man in the jumbo jet. Revelation therefore changes what we believe about a person or situation, and that changes everything else. Revelation moves you from information to understanding.

As we have come to realize that thoughts are things, it is easy for us to see that revelation is a resource. Rich people say that real money is an idea. It is the idea that attracts its material equivalent. In the same vein, revelation is a convertible resource.

"And the word became flesh…"[1]

In the story of the creation in the Bible, God used revelation as the basic resource for creating things. The Bible is filled with stories of people who achieved outstanding feats because they had access to revelation. Based on revelation, Abraham moved out of his country and became the founder of the nation of Israel.[2] Isaac got unusual yield on his own farm in a foreign country and prospered more than the citizens.[3] Jacob became more prosperous than his greedy employer who had reviewed his salary downward ten times.[4]

How to get revelation

The source of revelation is God. It is therefore helpful to cultivate a relationship with Him. Proximity is the key to intimacy. We need to spend time with Him. At first, it may seem awkward to converse with someone we cannot see. With time, when we become used to those spontaneous thoughts that He introduces into our minds, we long to communicate with Him. Spend time in meditation and prayer. Take time to read the Bible. You are tuning in to heaven's frequency. Always have your writing materials handy.

After I suffered a major disappointment in 1989, I was in an extended time of prayer, asking God for direction for my life. This was in January 1990. Then these words were impressed on my heart; "I will take you to Lagos to pastor a branch of your church, and I will bless you there." Those words were so real to me that a few weeks later I took off for Lagos. While I stayed with an acquaintance, I got a job offer but did not feel comfortable taking it. My heart was tuned to get an instruction from God. Then I got these words while in the car with my hostess; "Can you see poor people in Lagos? If you come here before I ask you to do so, you will suffer." I took my bag and went back to Ilorin in the middle belt of Nigeria, where I lived with my parents. Eventually, it happened just like the revelation said. In June 1990, my church posted me to pastor a branch church in Lagos. I arrived in the city with very few belongings and, needless to say, things have changed a lot. The revelation has become reality.

In prayer, we direct our thoughts, words and emotions towards God. Prayer is a dialogue, not a monologue, He responds. What comes from God to us is revelation or wisdom or an idea. If we accept it and build our words and actions on it, it eventually produces its material equivalent in our lives. Meditation is also very important. Meditation is deep thought. It also means to mutter to oneself. Really, it is thinking deeply to the point where you forget the world around you. It is good to meditate using the Bible as a guide. It is our book of possibilities. In it, poor people became prosperous, slaves got their freedom, the sick were healed and the dead were raised back to life.

We must appreciate that it is in the realm of thought that we make contact with the unseen world. We must set apart time to commune with God if we want to make meaning of our world and of our circumstances. It helps to know that we can maintain that contact all through the day.

12
ASSOCIATION

There is something called group thinking. The quality of your thinking, generally, does not appreciate beyond that of the people you relate with closely. That is why the Bible says; *"He who walks with wise men will be wise, but the companion of fools will be destroyed".* [1] That is the impact of group thinking. That is why it is important for you to deliberately move towards people who have already become what you want to become. It makes life cheap. It makes success possible and makes it come quicker than it would have come if you had to do it on your own.

Celebrate success

Let me give you some advice: do not criticize success; learn from it. We have to stop the attitude in some parts of the world where people believe that everyone who is getting outstanding success must be using some evil powers. There are good people who are succeeding legitimately. In many situations, the successful person is using information that is not available to others. Information is the best 'charm' to use, you know.

When Jesus recruited His disciples (or *protégés*), He said: *"Follow Me, and I will make you fishers of men."* [2] He did not say "I will teach you," but *"I will make you."* There is tremendous power in mentoring that transforms you into the kind of person your mentor is. The result of mentoring is not just information; it is formation. Anyone who can influence your thinking can influence your life. The major difference between rich and poor people is the way they think. The same situations rich people turn into money are the situations that make others poor. The difference is thinking.

I realize that a lot of people are afraid of change. When they move close to a mentor and the mentor suggests that they consider new perspectives, they become fearful and feel threatened. Mentors stretch your mind. They recognize your potential faster than you do and challenge you to release your potentials. They know that one of the greatest gifts you can give a man is a new perspective.

The example of Jesus

Now when they saw the boldness of Peter and John, and perceived that they were uneducated and untrained men, they marveled. And they realized that they had been with Jesus. [3]

Since they lacked formal training, the disciples of Jesus were not supposed to achieve the outstanding feats they were achieving. The elders and rulers of Israel marveled at Peter and John. They were looking for the key to the transformation of these common fishermen. Their conclusion was that these men *"had been with Jesus"* This scripture suggests that mentoring can help you overcome the limitation of lack of formal education.

These men were uneducated and untrained; yet, within three and a half years of being with Jesus Christ, they learned powerful things that transformed their lives. Jesus did not give them only natural information; He gave them supernatural information. They knew how this world operates, to the extent that they were healing the sick, raising the dead and opening blind eyes. They caused quite a stir. How do we explain this powerful transformation in the lives of these ordinary people? The only conclusion is mentoring.

Have a mentor

Like the disciples had Jesus as their Mentor, you too need a spiritual mentor. Your pastor could be your mentor. If you are in business, have a mentor in business. Whatever career you are in, have a mentor along that line. Have a mentor in marriage. Have somebody that you can ask questions.

The answers that you get sometimes for free can change your life altogether. If you are not sure of whom to emulate, ask in prayer. I believe God will lead you to a person whose relationship with you will change your life. What was difficult for you to do or acquire in the past will become very easy.

Everyone needs a mentor

As much you think you know, you do not know everything yet. The more you know, the more you know you do not know. There is always someone who sees the situation in another way that you may not have considered. Sometimes, it may even be someone who is lower than you in status. Do not be so proud that you cannot learn from others. "Let him that thinks that he knows know that he does not know as he ought to know. [5]

Life will be exactly the same as it was in the past without a change in your thinking. You need to read a book you have not read before. God is bringing fresh and life-changing information to you, and the avenue is mentoring. God will bring someone across your path who has passed through all that you are passing through; somebody who has succeeded where you want to succeed; someone who will show you the way. Where that person's success ends is where yours will begin.

SUCCESS
IS HOW
YOU FEEL

13
FEEL SUCCESSFUL

Imagine a guy; call him John, who comes into his house, tired from working all day. He lies on the couch and tells himself: "I just can't see anybody anymore today; I have to get some rest." But just then the doorbell rings. "Who's there?" He wearily calls out, almost angry. "It's me Janet," replies his fiancée. Mind you, John is tired all right, and sure needs some rest. But could he be so tired to lock out his beloved fiancée? What do you think will happen? The guy most surely would jump up with a new gust of energy. His tiredness would disappear, because his sweetheart is here! We are actually in control of our emotions at all times.

The human system runs on emotions. The nervous system in every human being is actually an electrical system that conducts small charges of electricity. Just think about that! As human beings, we are wired up just like a building. But if there were no electric power flowing through the cables in the building no appliances would turn on. The lights will not come on; neither the stereo set, nor the TV. The same applies to our physical system; it works with emotional energy. Understand that the flow of this energy or emotional power, largely determines our state in life. That is why it is important that we gain control of the flow of our emotional energy. Our emotions can be either positive or negative. We have to be able to identify which emotions are negative and which ones are positive, because negative emotions are destructive. We must be sensitive to our emotions.

The human system causes the body to malfunction when it is full of negative emotions. The glands release hormones in excessive quantity. On the other hand, the human system functions best when we run on positive emotions. "A merry heart," the Bible affirms, "does good like medicine."[1] *Positive emotion aids good health while negative emotion destroys one's health.* When the glands secrete hormones in excessive quantity, the hormones begin to wash the linings of the stomach, run through the intestines and create ulcers and all kinds of problems. Truly, we thrive on positive emotions.

Some people do not even attempt to gain any control over their emotions because they simply do not believe their emotions can be controlled. Some people can identify their negative emotions, but choose rather to avoid pain, and by leaving their negative emotions to fester, ultimately they are hurt. Negative emotions are not altogether bad; they are regulators. If we can interpret them accurately whenever they show up and become sensitive to them, they can actually be channeled to achieve positive things.

A negative feeling is a signal that something is wrong and that it requires attention. If you unconsciously touch a piece of electric wire that has a live current in it, you would quickly withdraw your hand to escape death. Thank God for the nervous system and pain, without which you will not realize the need for you to withdraw your hand and to stop the electrical process immediately. But for pain, for example, we would not realize the need for us to withdraw our bodies from fire. So, negative feelings are not altogether bad; they are regulators that help us realize when something is wrong.

Feelings create magnetic fields
Feelings create magnetic fields around our lives. If you are scientifically inclined, you must have been taught that there is a connection between electricity and magnetism, and that electric currents sometimes (given the right situation) create magnetic fields. Since our nervous system is the human electrical system, when emotions run through our lives they create magnetic fields.

Every magnet has the power to attract and to repel. *The kind of emotion that runs in your system will determine what you attract and what you repel. What you radiate determines what you attract or repel.* If you allow negative emotions to run through your life, you will create a negative magnetic field around you and attract problems while repelling opportunities. *"All the days of the afflicted are evil,"*[2] the Bible says. Who is the afflicted but the person who is feeling sorrowful, frustrated, sad, depressed and disappointed? Many people think it is just normal that we should feel negative when circumstances are negative. They believe that circumstances are to always dictate our feelings. However, it does not work that way only. It is our feelings, actually, that determine our circumstances.

The measure of your emotional strength

I like to put it this way: *it is not because things are bad that you are sad; you are sad that is why things are bad.* Take the control away from circumstances and put it in yourself. It is all about you. Some people would say, "Oh sure, when everything is working fine, I will be happy." You cannot afford to wait until then, because things may not become better at all. Take control of your feelings and emotions. *If your joy withers, everything else around your life dries up. Everything follows your emotions.* We are told,

The joy of the Lord is your strength.[3]

The more joyful you are, the stronger you are. The less joyful you are, the weaker you are. It affects every area of life. I like the way the following passage addresses the issue.

> Because you did not serve the LORD your God with joy and gladness of heart, for the abundance of everything, therefore you shall serve your enemies, whom the LORD will send against you, in hunger, in thirst, in nakedness, and in need of everything; and He will put a yoke of iron on your neck until He has destroyed you. [4]

Is that not terrible? *Negative emotions attract poverty and repel prosperity.* This text explains one of the causes of poverty. *Blessings are reversed when there is no joy.* The text says that God Himself will send those enemies 'in hunger, in thirst' (hunger and thirst sum up poverty). God even takes the poverty to a new degree: 'in nakedness and in need of everything.'

I pray you will not lack. But the secret is to get excited. Get enthusiastic about life. Take control of your emotions to your own advantage. That is why *we cannot wait until circumstances change before we get excited. Our destinies are tied to our joy.* We have to take control of our emotions because in the first place, it is the state of emotion that determines the state of everything else around our lives. That you lost a job is no excuse for sadness. That things are not working is not a good reason to sorrow. There is an exciting passage you should make your personal confession when things seem to look down.

> Though the fig tree may not blossom, nor fruit
> be on the vines; though the labor of the olive may
> fail, and the fields yield no food; though the flock
> may be cut off from the fold, and there be no herd
> in the stalls; Yet I will rejoice in the LORD, I will
> joy in the God of my salvation. The LORD God
> is my strength; He will make my feet like deer's
> feet, and He will make me walk on my high hills.[5]

Agreed, they fired you. Agreed, you just lost a business. Agreed, you just lost your money. You must not lose your joy also. Choose to be joyful. That takes the control of your emotions away from situations and circumstances and puts it within the realm of your control. *We experience frustrations in life when we try to control the things that we cannot control.* I have discovered that as far as emotions are concerned, they are within our control. Take charge and take control.

The testimony of faith

I remember the story of a military officer who lost his job. He was so highly connected that he felt that he should have known first-hand that he was going to be retired. However, no such information got to him. The military was reviewing the list of its personnel at the time. He was sure that his name was not on the list of those to be retired. But by the time the list came out in the newspapers, his name was there. Retired!

Our retiree got home that Friday night and tried to weigh things vis-à-vis the clear message God told him earlier that he was about to get a promotion. He told himself, "Well, this must have to do with the promotion God was talking about." At home, he put his musical cassette (in those days) into his stereo set and set it to continuous play from that Friday night till Saturday morning. He sang and danced. A friend came to visit him the following day. "Is it true that you've been retired?" She asked. "Sure," he replied unperturbed. She burst into tears, but he quickly stopped her. "God told me He's giving me a promotion," he assured her. "This must be the promotion he's talking about. I'm excited." From then on, his attitude set him up for a miracle, because he did not allow the situation to make him create a negative magnetic field around his life. Since his retirement was to take effect after his terminal leave, he spent the time maximizing his service to God. Then, he received a top job offer from a firm. When he got his letter of appointment, he saw that the date of resumption was exactly the effective date of his retirement from the Air force. He did not lose a single day. Secondly, he said that during the period of the terminal leave he got his highest income in a month. His new salary was much more than his former salary.

If you got a letter saying you were fired, and you now go about with a long face, you may be driving away your miracles. Let the joy of the Lord be your strength. *Do not give any situation or anybody the permission to make you frustrated and sad. Negative emotions attract problems and repel miracles.*

The exciting emotion of faith

Faith is an emotion: an emotion of confidence, competence and possibility. It is important we cultivate confidence. As soon as your mood begins to go low, track it. When your battery is going low, you do not leave it till you cannot move your car. You know that soon the car will not start anymore.

Keys to taking control of your emotions

KEY 1: Identify what you are really feeling:

You need to be conscious of your emotions. Do not go into mood swings without understanding the root cause. Track the thought that triggered the emotion. Could it be a negative statement somebody made, or something negative that happened? Could it be something that is not even true yet? Seek to preserve a positive atmosphere around your life. God is spoken of in this wise:

**In Your presence is fullness of joy; at Your right
hand are pleasures forevermore.** [6]

Every being has an ideal environment where they function. Even
God does. God thrives in an atmosphere of joy and celebration.
*The Spirit of God is stifled in an atmosphere of grief, sorrow,
bereavement and depression.* He seeks to turn our mourning into
dancing. Let us identify some negative emotions.

Anger

We feel angry when we have been prevented from achieving a
goal, or our values and standards have been violated. While anger
itself is not bad, it can easily spin out of control. Then it becomes
destructive.

Fear

There is natural fear, the kind you feel if you come across a bear
in the forest. It causes a rush of adrenaline so you have the power
to escape danger. But there is the negative emotion of fear. Fear
of failure is perhaps the one most people are familiar with. The
next one is fear of criticism. Fear paralyzes initiative. Fear stifles
the imagination. It kills creativity. So deal with fear. The bible says,
*"God has not given us a spirit of fear, but of power and of love and of
a sound mind."*[7]

Rejection

Rejection is what you feel when you are not wanted by someone.
It destroys self-esteem.

Frustration

This is the feeling of defeat, of resignation.

Hurt

Hurt or pain usually comes from our human relationships.

Guilt

This is a feeling of remorse or regret over a particular action you have taken. Guilt is destructive. It kills. If you will ever overcome guilt, you have to learn forgiveness.

You have to learn to receive forgiveness from God; you have to learn to forgive other people, and you have to learn to forgive yourself.

Depression

This is when your emotion sinks low. You cannot be depressed and inspired at the same time.

Grief

This is a feeling or sense of loss or bereavement.

Loneliness

Loneliness is the feeling of being alone without friends or companions.

Inadequacy

This is when you feel you cannot do something you want to do. You feel you just may never be able to do it.

Anxiety or Worry

This is when you feel negative about something that has not happened. It is expecting the worst to happen.

KEY 2: Find out why you are feeling that way

Finding out why you feel the way you feel helps a great deal. For a long time I thought being a man meant not expressing one's emotions and giving in to no sentiments at all. But let me share with you the story of a man who never lost a single battle and was a warrior all his life. He was one of the greatest leaders of all time yet he cried when it was necessary to cry. His name was David, an ancient King of Israel.

I think real men actually express their emotions when it is necessary while still exercising control over those emotions. When David was afraid, he said so. When he was angry, he said so. I think the key thing was that he was in touch with his emotions. Some of us avoid or pretend about our emotions as if they are not there until we suffer nervous breakdown. David asked a question:

> **Why are you cast down, O my soul? And why are you disquieted within me? Hope in God, for I shall yet praise Him for the help of His countenance.** [8]

Why am I depressed? Why am I crying? Why these negative emotions? Why the discouragement? Find out why you feel the way you feel. It may be because you want to achieve a goal but someone has obstructed your path and made it difficult for you to achieve your goal. Alternatively, you may be feeling the way you are feeling because of something that happened in the past. Sometimes, the person who offended you has asked for your forgiveness. By the time you track exactly why you are depressed you are usually able to quickly deal with it. If the person had asked you for forgiveness, then there is no point crying over spilt milk. There is no point feeling bad about something that happened in the past that you can do nothing about. Moreover, if you really think about it, you may be feeling bad about a wrong assumption.

You know, some of us give in to the weaknesses of our temperaments or personality types. Some people get signing bonuses at their jobs. Some people get furnished homes. Why worry about something that has not yet happened? Jesus addressed that when He admonished us not to worry about tomorrow: *"Sufficient for the day is its own trouble."* [9] He was saying that *what looks like a problem to you today may have changed by the time tomorrow arrives.* It would no longer be a problem. So why worry?

KEY 3: Pray, meditate and give thanks to change your emotions
The first thing to do when your emotions try to go negative is to pray.

> **Be anxious for nothing, but in everything by prayer and supplication, with thanksgiving, let your requests be made known to God; and the peace of God, which surpasses all understanding, will guard your hearts and minds through Christ Jesus. Finally, brethren, whatever things are true, whatever things are noble, whatever things are just, whatever things are pure, whatever things are lovely, whatever things are of good report, if there is any virtue and if there is anything praiseworthy--meditate on these things.** [10]

These verses changed my life as a young man, and they are still a blessing to me. Be anxious for nothing: not over your marital situation, not over a child, not over your financial situation. It is when you lose your joy and your peace that the real problem begins. The first thing that would happen before God changes your circumstances is that He would change your emotions. For Him to try to put miracles in your life when you still have a negative magnetic field around your life would be conflicting. Prepare for your miracles. *A positive attitude is not a gift. It is a choice. Make that choice right now, to be happy no matter what.*

KEY 4: Take action

What should be our first action towards those who offend us? **We should forgive.** Forgive the person who offended you. Jesus taught us to pray, *"Forgive us our sins as we forgive those who sin against us."* [11]Also, forgive yourself if you are the one who offended God or if you are the one who offended yourself. Sometimes, people break set high standards and find it difficult to forgive themselves when they break those standards. I have stated that negative emotions are not that bad; they are just signals to let you know that something is wrong. The second action is to **Love.** Choose to walk in love. The third action is to get excited: sing, dance, and celebrate!

Positive emotions to encourage

1. **Love:** Love is the primary nature of God. Choose to see good in others and let it reflect in the way you treat them.

2.**Thanksgiving:** An attitude of gratitude. Switch over to thanksgiving. Things are not as bad as you think. You are still alive and that is why you can complain about not having money. If you were dead, even if someone gave you ten million dollars it would not matter. Thank God that you are alive.

3. **Determination:** There is power in a made-up mind.

4. **Faith:** Think possibilities only always.

5. **Vitality:** This talks about your physical health. You must agree that your health affects your emotions. It is difficult to feel excited when you are sick. That is why it is good for you to maintain sound health. Take exercises. Eat good food. Feel good. More importantly, find time to rest and relax. *If you do not deliberately find time to rest, you may soon be laid to rest.*

6. **The feeling of contribution.** This last one is the ultimate. It is what you get when you add value to other people's lives. It is difficult to describe, but when you taste it, you would find out that money couldn't buy it. There is no amount of money you would have in the world that can give you the kind of fulfillment you get when you add value to people and you watch their lives change literally right before your eyes. It is awesome!

When you give, it is given back to you, *"good measure, pressed down, shaken together, and running over."* [12] It is not so much the fame; sometimes that is one of the by-products; and not so much the money or material things, though they are part of the by-products. It is rather the feeling that you have impacted another person's life that is just so wonderful.

Finally, you need to develop emotional flexibility. This is very critical. It is the readiness to change if it is not working the way you are going about it. If you do not allow yourself some flexibility, you will be frustrated almost every day of your life. Be the kind of person that is open to other ideas. Emotional flexibility gives you the capacity to adapt as the environment around you changes.

SUCCESS
IS WHAT
YOU SAY

14
TALK
SUCCESS

One of the most powerful resources with which we create success is the spoken word. There is creative power in words. According to the biblical account of creation, God literally spoke this world into existence. Given that man was created in the image of God, we also have the capacity to create our individual worlds with words. In fact, Solomon, the wise king in the Bible, said; "Death and life are in the power of the tongue; and those who love it will eat its fruit."[1]

Words are seeds

Words are seeds. The realities of our lives today are to a large extent harvests from the seeds we sowed with our mouths yesterday. Realities of our lives tomorrow will be harvests from seeds we are sowing with our mouths today. You only need to hear people speak to their spouses or children, or about their situation, and you will understand the root of their good or bad circumstances. I hear rich people talk in terms of abundance and I hear poor people talk in terms of scarcity. We can literally change our lives by changing the kind of words we speak. I know that may not be easy sometimes, but it very possible.

I was a young graduate, still trying to get a job when I began to tell people around me that I was not a local champion, and that I was going to make impact around the world. It sounded ridiculous but it is happening already. When people heard me say that I will not be broke again for the rest of my life. They probably thought I had a stack of cash stashed somewhere, but I was only using the concept of a principle. What you say is what you see. It is unfortunate that many turn this principle on its head; what they see is what they say. They talk too much about their challenges. We must set new standards for the words that we speak.

It was tough at a time for us to pay our bills in the office, and it became common for us to remind staff that there was no money. When I realized that we were breaking a law of success, I put a ban on that statement. In a short time we were out of that predicament.

Words are Vehicles

Words are also vehicles that convey resources from the intangible world to our material world. Words establish the contact points between our dreams and reality. We cannot afford to speak words carelessly. The invisible and visible worlds are controlled by words.

To Alter Your Life, Control Your Tongue

Human language has been terribly corrupted. We easily speak words of doubt, defeat, lack, difficulty, pain and failure, and we mix them with negative emotions. The result is almost certain to be negative. To change the direction of a ship we must take control of the rudder. To alter the direction of our lives we must take control of our tongue. Jesus said:

> **"For assuredly I say to you, whoever says to this mountain, 'Be removed and be cast into the sea,' and does not doubt in his heart, but believes that those things he says will be done, he will have whatever he says."[2]**

We must speak words with authority to get meaningful results. You are your own prophet and whatever you say is coming to pass.

SUCCESS
IS WHAT
YOU DO

15
ACTION ORIENTATION

The laws of motion help us to understand that nothing moves in our physical world until we move it. If you see anything moving on this planet, there is a force that is moving it. From the previous chapters, we have learnt a lot about how to move things internally: how to move our thoughts and emotions, how to dream, and how to plan. But now we have to focus on how to turn our dreams into reality. Action bridges the gap between dreams and reality.

Action as proof of faith

Thomas Edison is claimed to have said that success is one per cent inspiration and 99% perspiration. It is good to listen to inspirational talks on audio; it is good to read books; it is good to attend seminars; it is good to be fired up and inspired. But after all of that, you must do something. *If you do not take action, your dreams will remain realities in the invisible world.* Faith without a corresponding action is dead. In other words, *lack of action kills dreams. The proof that you believe something is in your doing it. If you don't do it, you don't believe it.* You will do the things that will bring you the millions if you believe that you are a millionaire. If you believe that you will get a job, you will go where the job is and do whatever you have to do to get the job. I am encouraging you to be an executive.

I always thought an executive was someone dressed in suit and tie, carrying some briefcase about town: someone who drives around in a posh car and works in an air-conditioned office. That may not always be the case. 'Executive' is from the word 'execute'. An executive is therefore someone who knows how to plan, and knows how to execute those plans. The world will not recognize you for what you are planning to do but for what you have done. *There is no recognition for a dreamer whose dream has not yet become a reality.* The dreamers we recognize in the world are those who are fulfilling their dreams.

Be passionate about your dream

Oliver Wendell Holmes, a former US Supreme Court judge is reputed to have said; "Life is action and passion, therefore it is required of a man that he should share the passion and action of his time at the peril of being judged not to have lived." In other words, there are people who are breathing but who are not alive. Life is action and passion. You begin to take action the moment you are born; there is no time for rehearsals. Some people live their lives like they are preparing for another life to start for them.

What use is it rehearsing if you will not participate in the real play? Life is about action; it is about passion. Do not be a spectator in life; jump on the field and be part of the action. Time is running out and action is essential. Take advantage of the opportunities you have today. Do not procrastinate. Do it now. You only live once; you do not have a spare life elsewhere. Get the most out of every single day.

Be prompt and courageous

There is a time to dream, but know when to snap out of your dream state into reality. In January, some people say, "It's just the beginning of the year," as if it is not time yet to do anything. The year has started already. Almost 10% of the year is already gone by the end of January. Whatever you plan to do in the New Year usually starts on the first of January. You have to make things happen. There is one basic quality of heart that we need: courage. *Success is not for the weak. Success is not for the faint of heart. Success is not for fearful people.* You need courage to take action.

Courage is simply acting in the presence of fear. Without fear, courage loses its definition. The important thing is that you must not allow fear to snatch the initiative from you. Most successful people have fears like everyone else, but they act in spite of their fears.

Fear of failure

There are different kinds of fear that keep people from succeeding. Fear of failure is the biggest reason why people do not succeed. They ask, "What if it doesn't work out?" There are too many variables in our world. We do not live in a perfect world. So you cannot afford to wait until everything looks right so success is absolutely certain.

He who observes the wind will not sow, and he who regards the clouds will not reap. [1]

As long as you keep looking at situations and circumstances to decide when you are going to act, you will never get anything done. The circumstances may not always seem to be right. Ask, "What if it works out," instead of asking, "What if it doesn't work out?" The possibilities will excite you.

Fear of criticism

There is also the fear of criticism. Some always ask, "What will people say?" If you live in a community where there is a lot of mediocrity and poverty, that question is a big thing to consider. You know what? People will always talk! If you succeed, they will talk. If you fail, they will blame you. It is up to you to fulfill your destiny, and to give them something to talk about. So you had better get ahead with what you want to do. The only way to put critics out of business is for us to do nothing at all.

How to overcome fear

Now, you have to deal with fear if you are going to be able to progress. *Fear literally paralyzes initiative. It snatches from you the ability to act.* Fear kills your enthusiasm. It creates imaginary difficulties. That is why *someone described fear as False Evidences*

Appearing Real. Fear makes you to focus on the wrong questions.
Examples are: "What if it doesn't happen? What if you die? What if
it doesn't work out? I found out that *fear also frustrates self-control.*
One way to overcome fear is to be conscious of the infilling of the
Spirit of God.

**For God has not given us a spirit of fear, but of
power and of love and of a sound mind. [2]**

*Anytime fear takes over your heart and mind, remember that it is
not from God.* Fear is not from God. Fear is the direct opposite of
faith. *Faith is the key to miracles. Fear is the key to failure.* So do
not entertain fear in your heart. As long as you are filled with the
Spirit of God, tell yourself, "I do not have the spirit of fear. God has
given me the spirit of faith, the spirit of power, the spirit of a sound
mind." This way you run fear out of your thoughts and emotions,
because fear cannot survive when God is actively present.

Do the thing you fear

One thing you have to do to break the hold of fear is to do the thing
you fear. Usually, there must be some powerful miracle waiting for
you whenever the devil tries to scare you from taking action. Go for
it. Do it. *Bold action is the key to outstanding results.*

Some people want to wait till they feel like doing it. If you have to
wait till you feel like doing what you need to do to succeed, you
will be waiting forever. Do not wait till you feel like it. Amazingly,
the moment you begin to do it, you will feel like it. Take control of
your emotions. Whether you feel like it or not, do it anyway. You
do not have to feel like breathing yet you breathe. So, do not wait.

Do what you need to do now.

Be focused

I have a few suggestions. If you are going to take action, then do just one thing at a time. I mean that you should be focused. *It is concentrated, focused action that produces or guarantees results.* When you check the stonecutter, sometimes he may give a stone one thousand hits before it cracks. But wisdom tells you that it is not the one-thousandth hit that cracked up the stone. It was all the hits dealt to the stone in addition to the last hit that caused it to crack. So you have to *learn focused and persistent action.*

Do more

Secondly, learn to go the extra mile. Give it what it takes and a little bit more. Give life 110%. Jesus said if someone forces you to go with him one mile, go two with him. [3] Whatever you are doing, whatever your line of business, do a little bit more than the average person around you. Do not think that laziness is going to get you anywhere. *It is only a lazy person who becomes a millionaire in his dreams, but refuses to lift a finger.* Wisdom should tell you that there is no point riding a car in your mind all your lifetime. You cannot fully enjoy it there. Bring the car down to reality.

Solomon, a wise and wealthy king in the Bible once said; "Go to the ant you sluggard! Consider his ways and be wise." [4] An ant, as small as it is, gathers its food in summer and does not become hungry during the time of harvest. What is the size of the brain of an ant? If an ant with a tiny brain has enough sense to produce its food, I should not be hungry.

Get someone to inspire you

Thirdly, I recommend, that you have a mentor, because when you take action and start that business, it is not always going to be as easy as you think it will be. When you are beginning to feel low and frustrated, you will have someone to inspire you to try again. That has been a great blessing to my life. A few years ago, when I found it difficult to get the attendance at our events beyond a few hundreds, I attended large conferences hosted by my mentor. There, I would see thousands of people and would say to myself, "It is possible." Without inspiration, you may lose heart.

Be flexible

The fourth thing you need to do, can be seen in the story Jesus told about a man who planted a tree and came back after three years to get some fruit from the tree. When he found none, he ordered that the tree be cut down. But the vine keeper said, "Sir, do not cut it yet. Let me dig around it and put in some fertilizer. Let us give it another year."[5]

Be flexible. Change the approach for success if it is not working. If you have tried and it did not work one particular way, change something. Try again, but change something while you are trying. Your goal should be fixed, but the process should be very flexible.

Have a backup plan

Let us put it this way. Act scared. Approach what you do as if something is going to go wrong. Be prepared in case it does not work exactly the way you want it. Have another plan you can fall back on.

Nothing good comes cheap

Let me conclude this way. Settle this once and for all in your heart. You will not get something for nothing. Your ability to speak in tongues, pray and call fire from heaven cannot substitute for the need for you to work, and doing the work hard. I see people who get frustrated with the principles of God. They do everything they need to do spiritually, but fail to act. After God has given you a dream, the next thing God expects from you is action. Mary the mother of Jesus told the waiters at a wedding,

"Whatever He says to you, do it."[6]

I have made up my mind that whenever I have an inspired idea, I will attempt it. I have tremendous respect for the person who tries but fails than for the person who does not try because he is waiting for the perfect time, or because he does not want to fail. Such people never achieve anything. So, strike while the iron is hot just like in hunting game, you have to know when to pull the trigger. Some people plan forever. "I'm planning to... I'm planning to get a store... I'm planning to start a business...." They keep planning and do nothing about their plans till they drop dead.

Do it now

So what are you going to do now? You want to save money this year? This is the year. Start saving money today. Walk into a bank and ask for the forms for a savings account. Find the address of a stockbroker, walk into the office or call on the phone and ask what the stockbroker has to offer. I am tempted by procrastination like everyone else. However, I have learnt to tell myself, "Do it now."

I have some wise sayings that inspire me. I tell myself, "Bite more than you can chew." It is common for you to hear that you should not bite more than you can chew. That makes sense in some circumstances. However, I believe that most of the things you want to accomplish are more than you can chew. So, bite more than you can chew and God will help you with the chewing. There is another one. People would say, "If you try it, you will face the music." I was happy when I heard someone say: "Face the music, then one day you will lead the orchestra." You know what? When you take action and get good results, people around who have been lazy, sitting on the sidewalk waiting, would look at you as a success story.

Walk into an office confidently or make a phone call this week. Contracts will not always come and meet you at home. You may say that you do not have connections. How do people make connections? Is it not by making friends? Go to the restaurants that rich people go, join a club or go to church and join a group. In fact, find out where the CEO of that company where you want to work eats lunch. Time your visit. Buy water and sit down at a table not far from the place he sits. Be ready to wait as long as it takes! Put on your best suit. When you meet the person, stretch your hand and shake his or her hand as you introduce yourself. Make a move. Be innovative. Do something.

A sage said you should not wait for your ship to come in. Rather, you should swim out to meet it. Well, the idea is that you should not wait for things to happen. You should make things happen. There is a miracle waiting, but until you make that first move, nothing will happen. The multiplication of loaves by Jesus makes interesting reading. [7] Jesus blessed the bread, broke it and gave it to His disciples, and His disciples to the people. There is a very important question in that equation. In whose hands did the bread multiply? Was it in the hands of Jesus?

As you read the passage carefully, you realize that nothing happened until the disciples were practically reaching out to people. The higher probability is that the bread multiplied in the hands of the disciples. *People who do not take action do not see miracles*, because faith without corresponding action is dead. *Faith without works is dead.* Talk is cheap (except if your business, like mine, is talking!). When it comes to the issue of succeeding, you take bold actions based on what you believe. *If you do not 'act like' it, you don't really believe it.*

Be it and have it

Success is first of all who you are, and what you do is a product of who you are. You 'be it', then you 'have it'. However, the requirement is that *you should begin to act as if you have it, then you will have it. If what you call faith is not affecting your behavior, then it is dead, impotent faith.*

Lack of action kills dreams. There are a lot of talented people in this world who languish in obscurity just because they fail to act on their dreams. They lack the courage to take action. Someone said, "Thinking without action produces no music." If you will ever hear any good music in this world, somebody has to take that guitar or piano or drum set, and do something. There are people's lives that are not producing any good music because there is a lot of thinking but no action.

Break the habit of procrastination

Henry Wheeler Shaw, famous humorist, is reputed to have once said that the greatest thief the world has produced is procrastination and he is still at large. We have not been able to arrest procrastination. *Procrastination is the thief of time.* I want to urge you to break that habit. A *destiny delayed is the devil's delight. The more you put off action the more you put off breakthrough. The devil is excited when you refuse to do today what you could do today. Each time you put off till tomorrow what you could do today, the devil is excited because you are delaying a miracle.* The devil is excited because he knows that tomorrow never comes. Today is the tomorrow you spoke about yesterday. *Whatever you told yourself you were going to do tomorrow, do it today.* Maybe you never thought about it, but the plain truth is, you will never live in tomorrow, because *whenever 'Tomorrow' arrives, its name changes to 'Today.' Whatever you are planning to do tomorrow, start it now.*

The world only moves for the man or woman who moves himself or herself. *This world has a way of aiding the person whose mind is made up, and who takes bold action.* When you act boldly, God will step in, and the results will be beyond your capability. Just do it. Try it. There is nothing you will ever do that will give you total assurance of success before you start: absolutely nothing. In this world there are many variables. There are many things that are subject to change. But you always have to believe that things are going to change in your favor. Take bold action expecting God to help you. A tomorrow person accomplishes nothing today.

Tomorrow is a post-dated check. It is not yet useful to you now. Yesterday is a spent check. It is useless to you now. Today is what you can cash at the counter of destiny. Cash it. Life is about action. Don't be a spectator. Get into the action. This world is not a soccer field where only twenty-two hefty men (or as it is these days, ladies too) run after an empty leather ball filled with air, with three referees also running up and down the field with them. You have several thousands of people in a stadium shouting, screaming and cheering the players. But only the players, coaches and club owners, and probably TV channels, share the big money. The world is not like that. Jump on the field. There is a place for you. Be the one others are watching. Create the music. Create the action.

The factor of risk

You must be willing to take risks. For some people, this world is too risky. Starting a business is too risky. But *there is nothing meaningful you will achieve without taking risks.* The greatest risk in this world is not taking a risk. To live is to risk dying. *To love is to risk being rejected.* To dream is to risk failing. What is a world without risks anyway! It will be a world devoid of meaningful achievements. *The greater the risks you take, the greater your success. You have to learn to take big calculated risks, trusting God to help you.* By the way, *if you have chosen to live by faith, faith is a business of risks.* By faith, Abraham ventured out not knowing where he was going.

> **By faith Abraham obeyed when he was called to go out to the place which he would receive as an inheritance. And he went out, not knowing where he was going.** [8]

That was a classic risk! Imagine what it's like for a married man to take his wife and other dependants, and all possessions, and to say;

'Sweetheart, we're moving.'

"Where to?" the wife asks.

"I don't know," he replies.

"Why are we moving?" the bemused wife tries to know.

"God said move, so we move," comes his cute response.

That is faith laden with big risk. *You are not going to achieve any meaningful thing without faith. With the eye of faith, you see tomorrow before it arrives. However, what use is your ability to see tomorrow if you would not begin to adjust your life today, so that by the time tomorrow comes you would take the best advantage of it. It is better to be prepared and not to have opportunity, than to have opportunity and not be prepared.*

The essence of visions and dreams from God is to cause adjustment in our lives such that by the time tomorrow arrives we can take action with maximum returns. Get an inspired idea from God and make a move. Start running. *If you are trying to get ready by the time you are supposed to be ready, you are already late.* Start moving. Do something. The amount of information you already have puts a responsibility on you to act.

Knowledge accurately applied is power

People say knowledge is power. That statement is only partly true. Knowledge is potential power. It is knowledge that is accurately applied that is power. If you know what to do, you are only a potential success until you act on what you know.

Sometime ago I was reading a book. At the end of chapter one, the author said, "Stop reading this book, do something now."

He even wrote there the names and addresses of some companies and their toll-free numbers. I said, "Well!" So I picked the telephone and began to call them. "Please send me your brochure." They did. I started doing something immediately. Procrastination steals time. Set yourself up for miracles. Be willing to take big risks. I know the devil is going to say to you repeatedly, "What if it does not happen? You too ask him the question, "What if it happens." You want to start a business and the devil says, "What if you fail?" You say to him, "What if I succeed?" May be the salary you are earning now cannot even buy a motorcycle much less to buy a brand new car. But if the new business you want to start booms the way you have calculated on paper, then you would be able to live your dream. You would be able to be the person you have always wanted to be. Yes! What if it happens?

There is no sound reason in the world why you should not succeed. Maybe you have convinced yourself that it is not people like you that break through big time. That is not true. Your disqualification is your qualification. God has chosen the foolish things of this world to confound the wise. God is looking for someone who is 'stupid' enough to act on His ideas. Peter looked at Jesus as he walked on water. Then he said, "Master, if it is You, just say come." And Jesus said, "Come." [9] Now, is that not a risk? Normally he should look at Jesus and say, "Well, it is people like Jesus that should be walking on water, not human beings like us." But Peter thought that if Jesus could do it, then he could do it too.

Have you noticed that rich people do not have two heads? They are human beings like you. If they are qualified, you are qualified too. God loves us all the same. All that some people see is that Peter sank while attempting to walk on water. But there was more to it.

There were fearful people inside the boat, who were thinking to themselves: "You'll see. You think those of us who sit here in the boat are stupid?" So when the man began to sink, for them it was like, " we told you so?"

Some people do not see in the story that Peter shouted, *"Lord, help me,"* and that the Lord did not tell him he took an unnecessary risk. The Lord helped him, pulled him out of the water, and they both went back into the boat. The two of them must have walked together on the same water where Peter had been sinking. *If you fail while trying, try again.*

Be persistent

Finally, if you are doing something, be persistent. If you do it and it does not work out, try again. You must have a good attitude toward failure. That you tried and failed does not make you a failure. If you tried and you failed, and you now fail to try again, that is when you are a failure. Failur*es are simply successful people who gave up too soon. Successful people are failures who refuse to give up.* That is the difference. You will not be the first person to make a mistake. *If you have books on success, but have none on failure, your library is incomplete.* Find a book that can help you to deal with failure, or else your journey will be terminated too soon. In fact, *the best way to increase your success rate is to increase your failure rate, because success is born out of failure.* Check it out. If as a professional soccer player who plays the position of a striker, you insist that you will only kick the ball towards the goal when you are absolutely certain you will score a goal, we will soon forget about you. You would notice, usually, maybe not all the time, that the team that makes most of the attempt at the opponent's goalpost gets more of the goals. *Success is born out of failure. Turn failure into fertilizer and plant the seed of your new vision in your past failure.*

Look into the yard of successful people and you will see the relics of ideas that did not work. Successful people, usually, do not tell you about their failures and their mistakes. That is why you assume their life is different from yours. You assume that there is just a magic wand they have, the Midas touch. You presume that anything they do just succeeds. Sorry! Go and ask them; you will be astonished at what stories of innumerable failed attempts you will hear.

Learn the lesson. Forget the details
You thought your last failure was the worst one in the world. Some people have committed bigger blunders than that. Learn the lesson, forget the details, and try again.

> **No temptation has overtaken you except such as is common to man; but God is faithful, who will not allow you to be tempted beyond what you are able, but with the temptation will also make the way of escape, that you may be able to bear it.**[10]

If you carry a negative attitude, you will not find the way of escape. You need to relax. You need to have peace in your heart. But *bear this fact in your mind, there is always a way.* I pray you find it.

You will succeed.

NOTES

INTRODUCTION
1. Schuller, R. (1984). *Tough Times Never Last But Tough People Do.* Random House Inc.

CHAPTER ONE
1. Proverbs 23: 7a
2. Proverbs 4: 23
3. Matthew 12:35 (Amplified)
4. Mark 11:23
5. John 3:2-3
6. John 3: 6
7. John 10:30-33
8. John 10:34-36
9. Psalm 82:6.

CHAPTER TWO
1. 3 John 2
2. Genesis 1:26-27
3. Matthew 3:17b
4. Matthew 4:3
5. Matthew 4: 4
6. I John 5:4
7. Luke 4:18-19

CHAPTER THREE

1. Matthew 12:33
2. Matthew 13:15
3. 2 Timothy 3:16
4. Genesis 30:37-43

CHAPTER FOUR

1. Hebrews 11:3
2. Chang, R. (2007). *Chemistry (Ninth Edition)*. New York, NY: McGraw-Hill. http://en.wikipedia.org/wiki/Composition_of_the_human_body_-_cite_note-0
3. Romans 12:2
4. 1 Timothy 6:10
5. Jeremiah 33:3
6. 2 Corinthians 10:3-4
7. 2 Corinthians 10: 5a
8. 2 Corinthians 10: 5b

CHAPTER FIVE

1. Tracy, B. (2000). The 100 Absolutely Unbreakable Laws of Business Success. Oakland, CA: Berrett-Koehler Publishers.
2. Habakkuk 2:1-4
3. 2 Thessalonians. 3:10
4. Matthew. 24:41
5. Matthew. 24:40
6. Ecclesiastes. 10:10
7. Ecclesiastes. 10:15
8. Luke 14:28-31
9. Proverbs 10: 22

CHAPTER SIX

1. Ephesians 1:17-18
2. Acts 2:16-17
3. Genesis 13:14-15
4. 2 Corinthians 4:4
5. John 6:5-7
6. Philippians 4:19

CHAPTER SEVEN

1. Genesis 11
2. Ephesians 3: 20
3. Genesis 15: 1-6
4. Genesis 17: 3-16
5. Genesis 20: 1-7
6. Genesis 21: 1-3
7. Jeremiah 33:3
8. Acts 2:16-17

CHAPTER EIGHT

1. John 8:56-57
2. Numbers 23: 19
3. Genesis 37: 4-9
4. 1John 5:4
5. Genesis 39-45

CHAPTER NINE

1. Isaiah 61:1
2. Matthew 4:4
3. Hosea 4:6

7. 2 Timothy 1:7
8. Psalm 42:5
9. Matthew 6:34
10. Philippians 4:6-8
11. Matthew 6:12(New Life Version)
12. Luke 6:38

CHAPTER FOURTEEN
1. Proverbs 18:21
2. Mark 11:23

CHAPTER FIFTEEN
1. Ecclesiastes 11:4
2. 2 Timothy 1:7
3. Matthew 5:41
4. Proverbs 6:6
5. Luke 13:7-8
6. John 2:5
7. Mark 6:41-44
8. Hebrews 11:8
9. Matthew 14:28-31
10. I Corinthians 10:13

Wherever you are on the success journey, LEAD is the right book for you. It is packed with ideas you can use right away to transform your life right where you are, and it will help you increase your capacity for success in geometric proportions.

In this book, you will learn how to:

- *Unleash your ability to inspire others*
- *Leverage on principles to develop character*
- *Solve problems better and faster than before*
- *Transform your family and organization*
- *Become a change champion in your nation*

FOR OTHER
TITLES BY
THE AUTHOR,
Visit www.samadeyemi.net,
www.successpower.tv

658
Ade
Success is who you are

932
Adeyemi, Sam

DATE DUE

63643499R00083

Made in the USA
Lexington, KY
13 May 2017